Verifying Spiritual Reality

Robert Traer

ICRL Press

Verifying Spiritual Reality

Published by ICRL Press, 2024
ISBN: 978-1-936033-46-1

Cover Image by ractapopulous via Pixabay
Cover Design by Robert Traer and Jeff Dunne
Book Design by Erin Dunne

For reproduction rights or other information, contact:

ICRL Press
info@icrl.org
P.O. Box 113
Sykesville, MD 21784

Amazing grace! How sweet the sound
That saved a wretch like me.
I once was lost, but now am found,
Was blind, but now I see.

Through many dangers, toils and snares
I have already come;
'Tis grace hath brought me safe thus far
And grace will lead me home.

John Newton, two verses of *Amazing Grace*

An Explanation

In quotes of persons describing a near-death experience or their research on near-death experiences, I have replaced the acronym often used for this phrase, NDE, with the full description "near-death experience." I've also used the phrase "spiritually transformative experience" in place of its acronym, STE; the phrase "after-death communication" instead of ADC; and the phrase "out-of-body experience" for OBE. Reading each of these phrases seems to me to express more fully the experience than simply recognizing the acronyms. I want to remind the reader (and myself) that we are referring to experiences that are wondrous, transformative, and involve relationships and communicating that are experienced as extraordinary. These are not simply events that happened. I apologize for replacing the acronyms, should any of the quoted authors feel the change was unwarranted or detracts from their written account.

Thanks

With gratitude to my former colleague and friend, Ramola Sundram, for her excellent proofreading and editorial suggestions, and to Dr. Jeffrey Dunne of ICRL Press for helping in so many ways to publish this book.

Contents

Life-transforming . . .

I was astonished when my father told me about his near-death experience during cardiac arrest while undergoing surgery. As physicians struggled to restart his heart, he *woke*[1] floating above the operating table, amazed that he could *hear* their anxious voices while *watching* them frantically trying to save his life. He then began to move rapidly through a dark passage toward a brilliant light, where he saw my deceased mother smiling and waiting. As my father came closer to her, he felt the intensity of the bright light streaming from behind her. He had an overwhelming sense of being loved unconditionally and wanted only to join her in this light. Telepathically she told him that it wasn't his time. He quickly returned through the darkness and awoke in his aching body.

My father had never heard of near-death experiences (nor had I when he shared his memory with me). He was embarrassed describing to me such a strange and unbelievable experience. As a scientist, he knew that either the anesthesia he'd been given before surgery or the cardiac arrest shutting off the supply of blood to his brain should have made him unable to have any conscious experience or memories. Yet, he wanted me to know that this vivid experience was the most powerful moment of his life.

My father was not a religious man, but his near-death experience left him unafraid of death. Also, I found the experience made him a more loving person. At the age of ninety, when a stroke left him unable to swallow, he told me "his time had come." He asked his physician to remove the IV that had been providing him water and nutrition, and he soon slipped into a coma. I was at his bedside three days later when he died peacefully.

I haven't had a near-death experience. I have, however, read reports about near-death and other extraordinary experiences—especially reports by scientists as astonished as my father was by these powerful events. Survivors were certain they had met deceased relatives or friends in a brilliant, colorful environment and had experienced unconditional love—from a Being of Light.

As near-death survivors return to their ordinary lives, many no longer fear death and have found a new sense of purpose. Survivors, who before their near-death experiences were committed atheists, have returned from the threshold

1 I use italics for words that are not measurably factual but are meaningful.

of death affirming a loving God or Light, as well as a continuing life after physical death. Religious persons after near-death experiences often do not become more active in their religious communities, but instead feel that their lives have become more *spiritual*—which is also the feeling of many survivors who were not religious. I began to wonder if these near-death experiences could be evidence of a continuing consciousness beyond death.

In *Verifying Spiritual Reality*, I offer accounts of near-death experiences and scientific studies of these experiences. I consider examples of extraordinary knowing verified by scientists and explore mysteries that continue to confound them: consciousness and subjectivity, our sense of purpose and meaning, and experiences of grace.

The materialist perspective held by many scientists, and taken for granted in secular society, is defined in the Meriam-Webster dictionary as believing: "physical matter is the only or fundamental reality and that all being and processes and phenomena can be explained as manifestations or results of matter."

Scientific support for acknowledging that consciousness cannot be explained within the materialist paradigm is presented in the Galileo Commission's recent report, *Beyond a Materialist Vision: Toward an Expanded Science*, which has been endorsed by over 90 scientific advisors from 30 universities. The report recognizes that most scientists assume "consciousness is nothing but a consequence of complex arrangement of matter, or an emergent phenomenon of brain activity but asserts this "belief is neither proven nor warranted."

The scientists participating in the Galileo Commission assert "there are well documented empirical phenomena that contradict this belief." Including "Veridical reports of near-death experiences with complex intuitions, perceptions, cognitions and emotions during well documented absence of brain activity." There are also "Veridical reports of non-local perception that were confirmed independently during such near-death-states of absent brain activity."[2]

A second scientific critique of materialism, *Manifesto for a Post-Materialist Science*, has the support of more than 550 "scientists, professors, doctors, and thought leaders." This Manifesto asserts:

"The modern scientific worldview is predominantly predicated on assumptions that are closely associated with classical physics. Materialism—the idea that matter is the only reality—is one of these assumptions.

"During the 19th century, these assumptions narrowed, turned into dogmas, and coalesced into an ideological belief system that came to be known as 'sci-

---

2 https://icrl.org/galileo-commission-report/.

entific materialism.'" This belief system implies that the mind is nothing but the physical activity of the brain, and that our thoughts cannot have any effect upon our brains and bodies, our actions, and the physical world.

"Conscious mental activity can be experienced in clinical death during a cardiac arrest (this is what has been called a 'near-death experience.' Some near-death experiencers have reported veridical out-of-body perceptions (i.e. perceptions that can be proven to coincide with reality) that occurred during cardiac arrest. Near-death experiencers also report profound spiritual experiences during near-death experiencess triggered by cardiac arrest. It is noteworthy that the electrical activity of the brain ceases within a few seconds following a cardiac arrest."[3]

Reflecting these scientific affirmations, I propose the hypothesis that near-death experiences and other life-transforming experiences verify a 'spiritual' reality. I begin by offering three vivid examples of scientists whose lives were transformed by their near-death experiences.

Dr. George Richie (1923-2007) recalls in his 1995 book, *Return from Tomorrow*, an out-of-body experience during his cardiac arrest in 1943 when he was in Army basic training at Camp Barkeley outside of Abilene, Texas. Richie was to be transferred to Richmond, Virginia for further medical training when he contracted severe double pneumonia. In the hospital ward, Ritchie was found to have no pulse, respiration, or blood pressure, and was pronounced dead. About 9 minutes later, "as a last resort, the doctor injected adrenalin into his heart muscle. Ritchie's near-death experience apparently occurred in the 8 or 9 minutes between when the ward man found his body and the injection with adrenalin."

Richie remembers *waking* up in the hospital morgue and realizing he'd missed his train to Richmond. He "rushed out of the rear door of the ward building and found himself *flying* about 500 feet in the air. He appeared to *fly* many miles eastward from the Camp's station hospital over the frozen Texas plains, passing over a town with multiple blinking caution lights and stopping at a city on the eastern shore of a large river, above an all-night cafe." Realizing that other people couldn't see him and that his *body* didn't interact with physical objects, he returned to the station hospital. There he "had an extensive near-death experience, visiting other realms in the presence of a Being of Light whom he identified as Christ."

Researchers who verified Richie's *flying* observations report: "The out-of-body portion of Ritchie's near-death experience is very unusual in that it involves the experience of being out of his body, traveling to a distant location

3 https://opensciences.org /about/manifesto-for-a-post-materialist-science?

(523 miles away) and seeing details of an unfamiliar area, apparently very accurately. What is most striking is that the location of the cafe from the likely station hospital door appears to be exactly due east, and the location of the blinking caution lights is also at this precise latitude.

"Indeed, the maximum deviation from the hospital to Vicksburg could have been only 0.6 seconds of arc, or 2900 feet over 523 miles of travel. The fact that three key aspects of Ritchie's account have likely correlates at the exact same latitude, occurring at widely spaced intervals, and that Ritchie reports having traveled east strongly suggest that his *flight* was an objective albeit unusual event."[4]

Psychoanalyst and psychiatrist Carl G. Jung (1875-1961) in 1944 had a near-death experience when he suffered cardiac arrest during surgery. He wrote that this extraordinary experience gave him "a glimpse behind the veil."

"The only difficulty is to get rid of the body," Jung writes, "to get quite naked and void of the world and the ego-will. When you can give up the crazy will to live and when you seemingly fall into a bottomless mist, then the truly real life begins with everything which you were meant to be and never reached. It is something ineffably grand. I was completely free and whole, as I never felt before.

"I found myself 15,000 km from the earth [as he later learned this was the height required to view the extent of the planet that he was able to see]. I saw it as an immense globe resplendent in an inexpressibly beautiful blue light. I was on a point exactly above the southern end of India, which shone in a bluish silvery light with Ceylon [now named Sri Lanka] like a shimmering opal in the deep blue sea. I was in the universe, where there was a big solitary rock containing a temple. I saw its entrance illuminated by a thousand small flames of coconut oil. I knew I was to enter the temple, and I would reach full knowledge. But at this moment a messenger from the world (which by then was a very insignificant corner of the universe) arrived and said that I was not allowed to depart and at this moment the whole vision collapsed completely."

Jung wrote that afterwards he was "wakeful each night in the universe," experiencing "the complete vision," but not "as an I." Instead, he was "united with somebody or something." As if in "a silent invisible festival permeated by an incomparable, indescribable feeling of eternal bliss, such as I never could have imagined as being within reach of human experience." He learned that:

4 "Investigation of George Ritchie's NDE OBE," updated February 18, 2010, https://www.selfconsciousmind.com/ritchie/.

"Death is the hardest thing from the outside and as long as we are outside of it. But once inside you taste of such completeness and peace and fulfillment that you don't want to return."[5]

Orthopedic surgeon Tony Cicoria, in 1994 at a lakeside family gathering, was calling his mother on a pay phone when a bolt of lightning passed through the phone line and struck him in the face. It knocked him backwards and left him unconscious. He felt, however, that he was *flying*.

He saw his body on the ground and said to himself, "Oh shit, I'm dead." He saw people converging on the body. A woman waiting to use the phone was kneeling over him, trying to revive his body.

He heard his mother-in-law screaming on the stairs as she came rushing down and went right by him towards his body on the ground.

"I could see and hear her, but she couldn't hear or see me. I began to walk up the stairs but as I looked at my feet they were disappearing. By the time I reached the head of the stairs I was a ball of energy. My body had disappeared. I kept moving and went through the wall of the building without feeling a thing. When I got outside, I saw my kids and had the realization that they would be O.K.

"Then a bluish-white light that I knew was absolute love surrounded me, and I felt like I was in a crystal stream of energy. I could see the rays of light passing through it, and the light had a sparkly appearance. I was able to see that this energy made up everything and flows through it. I remember thinking, I could measure this. (That was the scientist in me.) I thought, whatever God is, this is it. I had an enormous feeling of wellbeing and peace, as the highest and lowest points of my life raced by me. I had the perception of accelerating, being drawn up. But as I was saying to myself, 'This is the most glorious feeling I have ever had'—slam! I was back in my body."

Cicoria later learned that the woman who had successfully restarted his heart was an emergency room nurse. Her being immediately available, in a place far from any medical resources, seemed to him more than coincidental. Once conscious and back in his body, he said to her, "It's OK, I'm a doctor." She quickly replied, "Well, you weren't a few minutes ago!"

For a couple of weeks Cicoria had pain from burns on his face, but otherwise felt alright despite his cardiac arrest. After a few weeks, however, he was surprised to experience an "insatiable desire to listen to piano music." After buying a few recordings and finding he especially liked Chopin's music, he

5 Michael Grosso, *The Final Choice: Playing the Survival Game* (Stillpoint Publishing, 1985), 127-128.

next felt a craving to play this music. When a babysitter asked to store her piano in his house, which he again thought couldn't be coincidental, he agreed and started to teach himself how to play. Then he began 'hearing' unknown music in his head. "The first time, it was in a dream," he recalls. "I was in a tux, onstage; I was playing something I had written."

After waking and hearing the music playing in his mind, he got up and began writing down what he remembered. Then, whenever practicing Chopin, the music that he had heard in a dream, "would come and take me over." He found a piano teacher and began getting up at four in the morning to practice and write down the music he was *hearing* before going to work in the hospital. After work he was at the piano again. "My wife was not really pleased," he admits. "I was possessed."

Three months after his lightning strike Cicoria was convinced that "the only reason I had been allowed to survive was the music." He began to think he'd been given a mission "to tune in to the music from Heaven."[6]

Psychologist and author Oliver Sacks (1933-2015) interviewed Cicoria for an article published in *The New Yorker* magazine. Instead of suggesting Cicoria's near-death experience was a hallucination, Sacks said to Cicoria, "the music went through an awful lot of trouble to get here, so the least you can do is write it." Cicoria remembers, "I was so shaken by what he said, I went home and bought a Sibelius music writing program."

Cicoria spent the next seven months writing the music down and practicing the music that continued to come to him. A year later he performed at the Goodyear Performing Arts Theater at the State University College in Oneonta, New York. He also recorded a CD entitled *Fantasia: The Lightning Sonata*. He performed the "music from Heaven" knowing, from his experience, that hearing it "takes you to a place that is peaceful and wonderful." He said he hoped that sharing this music might bring others "peace of mind that there's something beyond this life."[7]

---

6 Tony Cicoria, "The Electrifying Story of the Accidental Pianist & Composer," *Missouri Medicine*, 2014 Jul-Aug; 111(4): 308, https://www.ncbi.nlm.nih.gov/pmc/articles/PMC6179476/.

7 Oliver Sacks, "A Bolt from the Blue," *The New Yorker*, July 16, 2007, https://www.newyorker.com/magazine/2007/07/23/a-bolt-from-the-blue.

Part I

Near-Death Experiences

Biophysicist, Joyce Whiteley Hawkes

Joyce Hawkes was engaged in cell research for the National Marine Fisheries Service and teaching in the Department of Zoology at the University of Washington when she had a life-transforming experience.

While in her home, a leaded-glass window falling off a mantel hit her on the head, knocking her unconscious. She had never even heard of near-death experiences, but while unconscious she traveled through a dark tunnel and was drawn to a light. At the end of the tunnel she was surrounded by the light as she was reunited with her mother and grandmother, who had been dead for many years. They seemed healthy and happy and Hawkes felt loved by each. Then she found herself facing a Great Light that had the form of a person but was taller and lacked clear features. Being immersed in this loving light was the most powerful experience she had ever had.

When Hawkes regained consciousness, she was initially persuaded by her scientific mindset that these memories of her experience were simply a delusion. Soon, however, she had more unusual experiences.

While visiting her favorite bookstore, she picked up Raymond Moody's 1975 book entitled *Life After Life: The Investigation of a Phenomenon—Survival of Bodily Deat*h. After buying the book and reading Moody's research on near-death experiences, she began to reconsider the profound feeling she had while she was unconscious.

A friend (also named Ray), who was trained as a podiatrist, had taught Hawkes how to improve her memory skills using deep relaxation and visualization techniques. One day, sitting in Ray's office and listening to a memory training tape while he was in another room, she projected her mind to where he was and *looked around*. When Ray returned to where she was sitting, she described what she saw in the other room, which she had never physically entered. Ray was astonished by her remote viewing and agreed to help her test her new psychic abilities.

They discovered that Hawkes could observe Ray remotely in another room as he examined a patient and, without hearing what Ray was saying, she understood both the patient's condition and Ray's recommended treatment. Also, if Ray thought of a particular color, she could accurately identify it. Hawkes began to research information about having a sixth sense and being able to view things remotely. Soon she joined the class of a local healer and learned how to meditate. She began to have visions of angels, animals, and even other galaxies.

Her teacher suggested she might be able to heal others, and when she began to assist him this proved to be true. When she touched an elbow or a shoulder, the person felt a warmth that reduced the stiffness or diminished the pain. Soon she began to see her own clients. As a healer who was also a highly trained biophysicist, she focused her attention on the cells in a patient's body.

With her teacher and two other students, Hawkes went to Mount Shasta to hike and meditate. While returning to Seattle they stopped at a Catholic shrine, called the Grotto, outside of Portland. As the others prayed in a small chapel, Hawkes discovered a cave with a statute of Mary, the mother of Jesus, holding his crucified body. Hawkes had no relationship with the Catholic Church and only childhood memories of the Protestant church she had sometimes attended with her parents. Yet, she felt moved to kneel on the bench before the statute of the sorrowing Mary. As she recalled the bliss and love during her near-death experience, she heard a woman's voice say, "You are called to heal."

Back in Seattle, she left her laboratory research position and dedicated her life to healing. She meditated daily and after years of practice felt that she experienced divine guidance. She traveled to Southeast Asia to learn from indigenous healers. Finally, with two decades of training behind her, she began to practice the cell-level healing that she had verified was both physical and spiritual.

Reflecting later in life on her near-death experience, she concluded that it created a connection between her and "something much, much bigger" than herself. "If it is a part of God," she wrote, "the Source of creation, the bond has never failed. I lost my fear of death, and with it, my fear of separation from the Source." She affirmed before her death that the Source and Healing Presence that had transformed her life are available to everyone.

Before her extraordinary experience, Hawkes believed there was no life after death. After her near-death experience, however, "the continuation of consciousness became an unshakable reality."[8]

Joyce Whitely Hawkes died peacefully in the fall of 2023 and is revered by those she taught to meditate and those she helped to heal.

8 Joyce Whiteley Hawkes, *Cell-Level Healing The Bridge from Soul to Cell* (Atria Paperback, 2006), 3-9, 142.

Neurosurgeon, Allan J. Hamilton

Allan J. Hamilton graduated from Harvard Medical School and eventually became the chief of neurosurgery and chairman of the Department of Surgery at the University of Arizona Health Sciences Center. He was a script consultant for the popular TV series, *Grey's Anatomy*.

In his 2009 book, *The Scalpel and the Soul: Encounters with Surgery, the Supernatural, and the Healing Power of Hope*, Hamilton tells his readers that he wants us "to feel the spiritual echoes," as he did when treating his patients.

He reports that in talking with patients facing death, almost all have described with wonder how peaceful they felt as they prepared to leave this life and *cross over*. Some of them have even said they felt like they were "coming home" after being away. Hamilton asks, "Might we not rejoice that eternal spirit can spring forth from intermittent, mortal life experiences? That these *souls* can enrich and educate us for our personal journey?"[9]

Near the end of his surgical career, Hamilton had an experience that convinced him near-death experiences were real and that a patient's conscious mind *continues* when the patient is *brain dead.*

A thirty-four-year-old woman was suffering from an aneurysm in her brain stem that was so swollen and near other blood vessels that surgery was very risky. If not repaired, however, the aneurysm would inevitably rupture and end the woman's life. After the patient was fully informed of the risks, she consented to go ahead with the surgery.

It required cooling her body to stop her heart, and then using a heart-lung bypass machine to oxygenate and pump the blood back into her body. Once the body was sufficiently cooled and her heart stopped the bypass machine would be turned off, ending blood flow to the brain. The surgeons would have only twenty minutes to clip the aneurism—so it would no longer receive blood flow and present a danger to the patient—before restoring the patient's blood flow while slowly warming her body.

The surgery was videotaped and the audio track recorded any comments made by members of the surgical team in the operating room. During the surgery a nurse in the room announced that she was engaged to be married. She

9 Allan J. Hamilton, *The Scalpel and the Soul: Encounters with Surgery, the Supernatural, and the Healing Power of Hope* (Penguin, 2009), 43-44.

described her engagement ring and her fiancé's proposal on his knees in a nearby restaurant where they were dining together. When a member of the surgical team asked where the ring was purchased, she identified the jewelry store as Johnston Fellows.

The surgery was successful. When the surgical team visited the patient in the recovery room, they were shocked to hear her say that she remembered hearing conversations among the team during her surgery. She heard a female voice mention her engagement and recalled that the ring was purchased at Johnston Fellows. She also remembered the name of the restaurant where the nurse's fiancé had proposed. In other words, while "clinically dead" because there was no blood flow to her brain and her EEG was flat, she not only heard a conversation but created memories of it.

Hamilton writes that none of the physicians and nurses on the surgical team, all of whom were highly trained in the science of medicine, had ever dreamed they might witness what seemed to be conscious awareness without measurable brain activity.

When Hamilton talked again with the patient, whose name was Sarah Gideon, he learned that Sarah as a child had attended Catholic schools. Currently, she only attended mass irregularly but prayed each night before going to sleep. She confirmed that she had never heard of near-death experiences.

When Hamilton asked if she had other memories from her operation, she identified correctly the hair color and eye color of one of the female nurses, who had entered the surgical room after the blood flow to her brain had stopped. Sarah also correctly remembered that the pump technician had a beard and that there was a tall African American female nurse present during her surgery.

Hamilton showed Sarah's EEG recording to two colleagues in neurology who regularly examined such printouts and asked them if there was any chance that this person could have been alive when the measurements were made. Each said the EEG readings confirmed brain death.

In Hamilton's last conversation with Sarah, she asked, "Did it ever occur to you that the reason I may have experienced whatever I did—whatever you and your colleagues are running around trying to prove —might just be a reflection of my faith?"

"I'm not sure what you mean," Hamilton replied.

"I believe in God so I'm able to join Him," she said. "You don't—or you worry that maybe you don't—so you can't."[10]

10 Ibid.,190-203.

Hospice physician, Pamela M. Kircher

In her 2013 book, *Love Is the Link: A Hospice Doctor Shares Her Experience of Near-Death and Dying*, Kircher recalls from a meeting of hospice workers: "We all agreed that it is not at all unusual for patients to be aware of the presence of dead relatives in the last few days of life. In fact, we even agreed that such experiences are one aspect of nearing-death awareness."

Kircher begins her autobiographical sketch by describing her own near-death experience as a six-year-old child, "when a leaking abscess in her throat led to meningitis. After her mother put her to bed, saying she would either live or die," Kircher had what later, as an adult, she would describe as a near-death experience.

As if telling the story of someone else, she writes: "The next thing the little girl experienced was suddenly, inexplicably, being in the corner of the room near the ceiling and looking down at a little girl in the bed. She was not surprised or frightened, even though nothing in her solid Midwest background had prepared her for an out-of-body experience. She was totally without pain and in perfect peace.

"She had the strong sense that she was surrounded by God. She did not feel like a boy or a girl or a child or an adult. She experienced the essence of herself—the soul that had existed before she came into her body and that would exist when this life was over. She felt strong and peaceful and totally connected with God. Looking down at the little girl in the bed, she was aware of the girl's pain and felt compassion for her. As she further contemplated the situation, she realized that she must be that girl, and then the experience ended.

"That little girl was me," Kircher writes, "and the experience totally influenced the path that my life would take. Partly as a result of that experience, I have come to understand how tiny the distance is between the world we think we inhabit and the world of the Spirit.

"What I have learned beyond a shadow of a doubt is that there is more to existence than the things we routinely see, touch, and feel when aware of only our physical surroundings. Talking with many people over the years, I have found that most people have some events in their lives that indicate this to them, and that often they repress these experiences because these experiences are beyond their understanding of how the world functions."[11]

At age six, Kircher did not experience God as an old man with a beard, or as having any kind of body, but instead as a comforting presence around her. She also experienced herself in a new and surprising way, as 'the soul that had existed before she came into her body and that would exist when this life was over.'

Kircher confirms on the basis of her hospice work and research that relatives or friends of a person who has died may experience the presence of their deceased loved one. "While after-death communications are common during near-death experiences and in the last phase of life, these visitations occur under other circumstances as well. People are often 'notified' of a death by the deceased person. After-death communications are quite common in the days or first few weeks after the death of a close relative. Most of these communications seem to have the purpose of reassuring the grieving relatives or friends. Finally, a visitation from a deceased loved one sometimes brings a warning or comfort during difficult circumstances."

She gives several examples. "Two hours before his mother called to say that his sister had died, a young man was awakened from a sound sleep by the unmistakable feeling of his sister's presence. She seemed to be at the foot of his bed as she told him that she had killed herself because she was in too much pain. She assured him that there was nothing that he could have done to prevent her death. She also said that she felt she was in a better place than she had been while in her body."

"A woman told of being 'notified' of the death of a good friend, who died some thousand miles away. Although people were telling her he was all right, she felt his presence and the clear certainty that he was dead."

Kircher also relates, "A warning from a dead mother saved another person from a car accident. As a man was driving his usual path to work, he distinctly 'heard' his mother (who had died two years before) tell him to take another route. Feeling a bit foolish, he did take another route. Later in the day, he heard on the news that there had been a ten-car pile-up in the fog right where he would have been that morning had he not taken the alternate route."

In addition, Kircher reflects on spiritually transformative experiences, which do not involve nearly dying, and yet are very similar to near-death experiences. From listening to many people's stories, she concludes: "First, and most important, is that near-death experiences and spiritually transformative

---

11 Pamela M. Kircher, *Love Is the Link: A Hospice Doctor Shares Her Experience of Near-Death and Dying* (Awakenings Press, 2013), 8-13.

experiences are two avenues to the experience of being in the presence of God. One is not more important than the other. They are just different paths. Each is a type of spiritual awakening. Second, it is easier for some people to dismiss their mystical experiences as just an unusual event than it is for those who have had a near-death experience to do so. Lastly, it is difficult to differentiate between a spiritually transformative experience and a near-death experience. Sometimes the mystical experience occurs in a terminally ill patient who has weeks or months to live."

She gives examples of spiritually transformative experiences that, like near-death experiences, have had life-altering consequences. A scientist who was a confirmed atheist felt certain "that when we die, all that we are returns to the earth. In his spontaneous mystical experience, he suddenly understood the Universe and knew that it is all unfolding in exactly the way that it needs to unfold for understanding to develop. He could see how everything relates to everything else and how truly beautiful and intricate that it all is. When the experience was over, he was a changed man."

Kircher also relates the story of a woman who "was already feeling very discouraged when someone told her she ought to kill herself because she was of no use to anyone. That evening as she was recalling the encounter, she suddenly found herself surrounded by a peaceful white light that seemed to imply she was very much worth having around. She said that the experience was very unexpected and unbidden on a conscious level. It was a life changing event, and she has never felt so despondent since."

One of Kircher's patients shared this story with her. "Before his near-death experience, he had the highest sales in the region; but he also had the highest rate of repossessions, because his customers had tended to buy automobiles that they couldn't really afford. After his near-death experience, he gave priority to customer satisfaction rather than selling as many cars as he could at the highest price he could." Kircher adds, "He had very satisfied customers with payments they really could afford. He was content with his lower income because he felt like a partner with the customer, sharing common goals. The lower income was somewhat difficult for him, but he understood as a result of his near-death experience that the new approach to salesmanship was essential."

"I honestly believe," Kircher writes, "that everything that happens in life is for a purpose that will ultimately serve our highest good, and that I am responsible to look for ways to be in alignment with that highest good. As I have met many people with near-death experiences, I have come to realize that this attitude toward life is extremely common among people with near-death experiences (although, certainly, not exclusive to them).

"Another long-term effect of near-death experiences," Kircher explains, "is an increase in psychic abilities. I have seen this development particularly in people who have undergone car accidents and were comatose for long periods of time." There is "an increased sensitivity to people's feelings and moods—which can be wonderful in close relationships, but which also can cause a lot of difficulty in public settings. People who have had near-death experiences are often so sensitive to the energies around them that they can easily get exhausted in crowds. By the same token, violence is very disturbing to the near-death experience survivor, even the 'ordinary' violence on television or in movies. Some people have difficulty holding down jobs because their minds and energies are so scattered by the violence they see."

"In summary," she writes, "there are many long-term effects of near-death experiences, some of which lead to a happier, more fulfilling life, and some of which may cause considerable conflict in the lives of the people who have had them."[12]

Kircher refers to God as Spirit and gives examples of both near-death experiences and spiritually transformative experiences that led to a new sense of purpose and meaning. We also saw this in the music that Cicoria experienced as coming from Heaven—music that became his mission in life to write and perform—a mission that neurologist Oliver Sacks foresaw and encouraged.

Kircher urges her colleagues to help patients accept their death. "My plea is for physicians to be honest with patients about their medical condition and for patients to have the courage to say, 'No more!' when in their hearts they know the ultimate outcome. So much important soul work can be done in those last few days and hours of life that it should not be wasted in an ICU trying to live for a few more hours or days.

"After talking with hundreds of people in the past several years, I am convinced that contact with alternate realities is the rule rather than the exception. Sometimes that contact takes the form of a near-death experience. More often, however, it occurs in the normal course of a person's life, when they are physically well.

"People in the last few days of life are also in the unique position of being in two worlds at once. While their physical world is declining, their spiritual world is becoming more active. What usually needs healing are their relationships. Sometimes it is difficult for people to allow themselves to die because the family members are so attached to them." This may be why, Kircher suggests, that: "Several people in my care have died when family members stepped out-

12 Ibid., 60-89.

side for a moment or two. It was as if, at some level, they wanted to die alone or to save the family members the experience of being present at their deaths."

She concludes: "As people become more comfortable with sharing experiences of alternate realities with each other, I envision the nonphysical gaining an important place in our understanding of how the world works. My firm conviction is that the physical has seemed so paramount because we have refused, by cultural agreement, to discuss or see the nonphysical. As that agreement breaks down and people begin sharing their experiences, the greater breadth of how the world functions will begin to become more apparent. We will see that we are all much more interconnected than we have heretofore thought."[13]

Kircher suggests that we are all living in these two worlds, a spiritual and a physical world, even if we are unaware of the spiritual world most of the time. When we have what we acknowledge to be an extraordinary experience, we usually *know* something we didn't know before—even though we are unable to explain how we came to have this new knowledge. Kircher proposes that extraordinary knowing involves a breach between the physical and spiritual worlds allowing information from the spiritual world to enter our experience in the physical world.

13 Pamela M. Kircher, *Love Is the Link*, 116-135.

Christian Physician, Reggie Anderson

A majority of the near-death experiences that have been reported to researchers are not explicitly Christian. Physician Reggie Anderson, however, testifies to his Christian faith in his 2013 book *Appointments with Heaven: The True Story of a Country Doctor's Healing Encounters with the Hereafter*.

At the beginning of his book he describes the loss of his childhood faith in God after the murder of six members of the Alday family, Anderson's close relatives. Yet Karen, a woman he began to date while in medical school, told Anderson that a firm Christian faith was necessary if they were to marry. Anderson knew he loved Karen, but he wasn't convinced he had the faith she demanded until he experienced what he identifies as a life-transforming dream.

While camping beside a beautiful waterfall, he read the copy of *Mere Christianity* by C. S. Lewis that Karen had given him. When he finished, he felt he had found the answers to his questions about Christian faith. He knew Lewis had respected scientific inquiry and coherent reasoning, yet Lewis had also affirmed his faith in the God of love he discovered in Jesus Christ.

Anderson also read through the Gospel of John, which Karen had urged him to read and that Lewis had mentioned in *Mere Christianity*. Then he fell sound asleep. He remembers his mind "tumbling, free falling, like the waterfall nearby," and then experiencing an overwhelming sense of peace. Suddenly, he was surrounded by colorful wildflowers, swaying back and forth with the wind. He was stunned by the intensity of their colors. As he inhaled, he experienced the cleansing fragrance of citrus and lilac. He heard a trickling noise and noticed a running stream of clear water flowing nearby.

His dreamlike experience was *more real* than his everyday life! And then he heard the voice of "someone he had once loved" and who had continued to love him. He felt the words resonating inside him, with a voice that was both compelling and comforting. When he looked for the speaker, he observed instead, moving toward him, the six members of the Alday family who had been murdered.

He couldn't believe what he was seeing, but then he realized they were there to lift the burden he had been carrying. Although no longer alive on earth, they were real and full of joy.

Among them was a human form, surrounded by a glow, who appeared ageless, unlike anyone he had ever seen. There was a glow behind the form, creating the effect of a bright halo. He knew it was Jesus, as in his mind he heard the words: "Reggie, why are you running from me? Your friends are here with me in paradise; you can stop running."

Jesus told Anderson he would marry Karen, and that they would have four children. He would become a doctor and practice medicine in rural Tennessee. And, yes, all this came to be.

Anderson describes his first experience with a dying patient. An elderly woman, she had asked him to hold her hand, saying, "I'm going to see Jesus, and I need an escort."

That night, Anderson says, he experienced "the veil that separates this life from the next" parting. Holding the woman's hands, he "felt the warmth of her soul" pass by him and the cool breeze that followed her departure. As he smelled the fragrance of citrus and lilac, he knew the veil had parted so her soul could pass through.

While accompanying many dying patients over the years, Anderson says he has "sensed Jesus on the other side, standing in heaven's foyer, welcoming the dead who are made whole again." He has glimpsed brilliant colors, heard amazing sounds, and breathed in wondrous scents of "lilac, citrus, freshly carved cedar, and baking bread." Anderson affirms that, "Heaven is more real than anything we experience here, for the sense of peace, joy, and overwhelming love is beyond description."

Anderson vividly recalls treating a young man named DeWayne in the ER, who had a stabbing wound in his chest. Anderson had inflated his lungs, but there was no blood pressure. CPR hadn't worked, so as a last resort Anderson knew he had to 'stab' the patient in his heart. As non-clotting blood entered the syringe, Anderson felt a slight brush of wind on his cheek. Then he felt the warmth of DeWayne's soul returning to his body.

The following day when Anderson visited his patient, he was surprised to hear him say that while unconscious he had watched and remembered Anderson's unsuccessful attempts to revive him before inserting the syringe into his heart. DeWayne also said he was scared he would die, until his granny came and held his hand. Anderson later learned from the family that his granny had died four years earlier.

Anderson acknowledges that not all deaths are uplifting. While treating Eddie, who had abused his wife and children and was known as a trouble-maker in the community, Anderson came to feel that Eddie was "truly evil." As Eddie was dying from his cancer, Anderson sat at his bedside, praying for him.

Eddie's eyes grew wide, and Anderson saw his fear. When his last breath came, it wasn't followed by the peaceful exhale that Anderson had experienced with most of his dying patients.

Suddenly, Anderson felt a darkness enter in the room. The lights grew dimmer and he felt the temperature drop. He smelled sulfur and diesel, and he found it harder to breathe. Convinced that evil had entered the room, Anderson quickly left and hurried to the restroom to "wash the darkness off" his hands and face.

Anderson concludes his book by describing how he received from heaven a reassuring message delivered to him by a near-death survivor. He had finished his obligation to the National Health Service Corps, and he and Karen had questioned whether God wanted them to remain in Ashland City or serve elsewhere. The answer was delivered by Eunice, a patient in her late sixties, who was taken to the hospital in Nashville after having a heart attack.

Several hours later Anderson received a call from the treating physician in Nashville, Dr. Wong, who said Eunice had died on the operating table. Wong and his resident had tried for at least an hour to revive her but failed. As the resident wanted to practice cardiac resuscitation procedures, Wong let him continue for another hour. Then, Wong said, after two hours without a heartbeat, and without any intervention by the physicians, her heart began to beat again.

Three days later Eunice awakened from her coma and asked to see Dr. Anderson. When he entered her room, he was surprised to see how well she looked. He listened carefully as she described her experience at the hospital in Nashville.

She remembered lying on the table while the medical team did something with her heart. As doctors and nurses were yelling and passing equipment back and forth, Eunice suddenly was somewhere else and felt more alive than she'd ever been. A sensation of total peace enveloped her. For the first time in three years, she didn't feel any pain and was even able to walk on her own.

She saw a path and walked along it to a stream where she felt the icy spray carried by the wind. She stopped to take a drink and found the water "as cold and fresh as an Alaskan stream," but sweet. Looking around, she saw an amazing array of colors.

As she continued around a bend in the path, she saw a horse-drawn carriage in the middle of a meadow. Beside the carriage she saw her deceased father, mother, and brother, as well as others she had known when they were alive. They greeted her warmly and asked her to tell Anderson to continue his medical practice in Ashland City.

Then, Eunice continued, Jesus came and sat down beside her. He asked Eunice to go back to assure Anderson that he was doing God's will and should stay in Ashland City, and that she would soon return to be with her family and friends.

Anderson easily combined his life as a scientifically trained physician with his Christian faith. His extraordinary experiences were subjective, but some of these were objectively verified. Dr. Wong of the catheterization lab in Nashville confirmed that Eunice was dead for two hours before her heart restarted. Other medical staff, as well as Anderson, verified that Eunice was lucid when she returned to Ashland City and delivered her message from heaven.[14]

---

14 Reggie Anderson, *Appointments with Heaven: The True Story of a Country Doctor's Healing Encounters with the Hereafter* (Tyndale House Publishers, 2013).

Hindu Anesthesiologist, Rajiv Parti

In his 2017 book, *Dying to Wake Up: A Doctor's Voyage into the Afterlife and the Wisdom He Brought Back*, Parti begins his astonishing account by describing his own experience as the anesthesiologist for a surgery to repair the tear in a patient's aorta. The patient's heart had stopped beating, and the blood was drained from the arteries connected to his brain.

The patient wasn't dead, however, but was being kept "alive" during surgery in suspended animation. The patient's blood had been replaced with a cool fluid to lower his body's temperature to almost 50 degrees Fahrenheit. This procedure stopped all bodily functions. Parti thought of this patient as the *frozen man.*

As the anesthesiologist, Parti's responsibility was to keep the patient unconscious while the surgeons opened his chest and operated on his heart. After warm blood was returned to the man's body and the ice around his head was removed, the surgeons used cardioversion paddles to stimulate the heart so it would resume beating. On the third try they succeeded, and the patient was moved to the intensive care unit.

When Parti visited the patient after he was awake, the patient surprised Parti by telling him that during the surgery he was outside of his body watching the surgeons from near the ceiling. Parti knew that couldn't be, because the man was frozen during surgery. Yet, the patient clearly described how a surgeon stitched a patch on his artery, the actions of the nurses, the surgical tools in the operating room, and the number of surgeons present.

The man wanted to say more to convince Parti he had watched his entire operation, but Parti ordered a shot of a strong antipsychotic drug that put the patient to sleep. The stock market had closed, and Parti wanted to check on his investments.

In 2020 Parti once again considered his conversation with the *unfrozen* man, after awakening in the recovery room at the Los Angeles Medical Center. He had undergone surgery for prostate cancer, and Parti was similarly eager to relate his own near-death experience to the anesthesiologist, who—Parti wasn't surprised to find—likewise wasn't interested in hearing about it and soon left him alone.

Before Parti's operation, his surgeon explained that he was full of pus from an infection in his abdomen that couldn't be treated with antibiotics. They had to clean out the pus before they could safely operate on his prostate gland.

After being anesthetized and becoming unconscious, Parti recalls being out of his body near the ceiling and observing the operation. He was also aware of the terrible smell in the room due to the pus being suctioned out of his abdomen through incisions made by the surgeons. One nurse was applying eucalyptus oil to the masks of the surgeons and other nurses to reduce the stench they were experiencing. When the anesthesiologist in the operating room told an off-color joke about the odor coming from Parti's abdomen, everyone laughed including Parti.

Suddenly, Parti felt his field of vision expand. He was shocked by the information flow, and some of the visions were unpleasant. He focused on the happy vision of his mother and sister sitting together in New Delhi. Parti tried to communicate with them and reached out to his mother, but his hand went through her.

Then he was moving through the darkness toward a storm and saw lightning and heard thunder. Suddenly he was at the rim of a flaming canyon, hearing screams and smelling the odor of burning flesh. It had been many years since in had lived in India and spoken Hindi, yet the word *Naraka*, the Hindi word for hell, quickly came to mind. He also recalled that *Yama* was the name of the Hindu god of death. He heard a voice say, "You have led a materialistic and selfish life."

Parti knew this was true. He lacked empathy for his patients and saw them only as a means to make him wealthy. He knew he had verbally abused family members, especially his older son. Standing at the edge of hell, he desperately prayed for another chance.

He saw his father coming toward him. Like many Hindu children, the only time his father or grandfather had touched him was to inflict punishment. Standing next to his father in the afterlife, Parti relived not only how he felt being beaten but also how his father had felt as he was doing the beating.

Yet, in the afterlife, Parti's father seemed to be someone who had looked "into the eyes of God." His father also looked younger and stronger than he remembered. He noticed his grandfather standing beside his father and he, too, looked younger and also had the "look of God" in his eyes. Parti saw that behind his father and grandfather was a line of ancestors, each of whom had been angry with their fathers.

Without moving his lips, his father said, "My son, if you are truthful to your own self, the God, the Divine, the Universe, will take care of you." Then

Parti's life review began. He saw childhood events that were innocent and fun. He heard a telepathic message from God, saying: "The simple moments are most important, because there are no simple moments. All moments build the person you are."

More visions flashed before his eyes before he focused on one. He was sitting in a courtyard in medieval India, watching the farmers who cared for his land and whose cheap labor had made him wealthy. He arose and, with several soldiers, began to whip the farmers. He didn't know why he was whipping them, but he realized he enjoyed striking their backs. Feeling how the motion of his arm hurt his wrist, he recalled that in his current life he had torn a ligament in his wrist. To dull the pain, he had taken pills and become addicted to them.

Appalled by his unjustified abuse of those who worked for him in this past life, he asked them for forgiveness. And they came to him, one by one, and accepted his apology. When some touched his forearm, he felt a flash of electricity, which he later believed had healed the recurring pain he had experienced in his wrist for many years.

Another life review began. He was in Afghanistan in the nineteenth century, the owner of an inherited field of poppies. He was rich but had become an opium addict. Parti realized that his current addiction to modern narcotics was no different than this addiction a century earlier.

He also recognized that in his current life, he was behaving as he had in these previous lives. Parti resolved that if his surgery was successful giving him a second chance, he would break these patterns and live more responsibly.

Once more he was in the dark tunnel, now heading toward a bright light. Two angelic forms hovered over him, explaining telepathically that they were the angels Michael and Raphael and would guide him. As Parti was familiar with the Bible, he was not frightened by their presence. It was only later that he learned Saint Michael is the protector of people and the angel who opens doors, while Saint Raphael is the angel of healers.

As Parti continued toward the light through a meadow of bright green grass and colorful rosebushes, he heard the sound of *om* as though being chanted by nature itself. He closed his eyes and tried to enter the state of *Shanti*—resting in pure peace and bliss.

Perhaps he appeared nervous as Michael said to him, "The higher you go up in the spiritual realms, the more formless it becomes." Raphael touched his shoulder and added: "You become surrounded by a powerful entity of energy, of pure love and intelligence, and this pure love is the base reality, the underlying fabric, of everything in the universe."

Then a Being of Light whispered in Parti's ear, and he felt the pure love that pervades everything. "I am one with the universe," he thought. The Being of Light told Parti he was to become a healer of the soul. He had experienced the diseases that "tax the soul" and would "show others how to resist these diseases spiritually."

Suddenly, Parti was in a clinic where natural light streamed through the windows. Patients were practicing yoga, and others were sitting in cross-legged meditation. All were concentrating on gaining spiritual guidance, and Parti felt grateful for the love surrounding him.

He knew he was returning to the operating room, and he felt as if he was driving through a dense white fog. He was afraid he would crash and die. Then he realized that the universe was in complete control of his life. He had nothing to fear.

When the surgeon and his resident visited Parti in the hospital recovery room, he began to tell them about his experience during the surgery. Soon, however, they left to visit other patients. His nurses were more receptive, for they often heard experiences like his. One of them told Parti that many patients see departed loved ones or mysterious Beings of Light, especially when during surgery a patient has a cardiac arrest or for some other reason nearly dies.

Parti's wife, Arpana, visited him in the hospital and listened attentively to the account of his near-death experience. She was surprised but pleased that he had reconciled with his father. She wondered, however, why he had met Christian angels instead of a Hindu god or goddess. She reminded him that he became an anesthesiologist because he didn't like to talk to patients, and she wanted to know what a change of vocation would mean for her and their children.

After Parti returned home, he meditated daily. There came a day, however, when sadness clouded his mind. He wondered if God was punishing him for being greedy and proud. Moreover, his loss of income and the reduced value of his investments, weighed on his mind. Then Michael and Raphael returned to tell him that drifting away from meditation was a common experience. They encouraged him to continue his practice and to trust that the power of the universe would guide him.[15]

On his web site at https://rajpartimd.com/ Parti describes his new spiritual healing practice.

15 Raj Parti with Paul Perry, *Dying to Wake Up: A Doctor's Voyage into the Afterlife and the Wisdom He brought Back* (Simon & Schuster, 2017).

Forensic Pathologist, Janis Amatuzio

In her 2004 book, *Forever Ours: Real Stories of Immortality and Living from a Forensic Pathologist*, Janis Amatuzio shares her personal experiences. She was in the final month of her internal medicine internship and in a hospital, where she had to work a thirty-six-hour shift and then was off for twelve hours. She had been asleep for thirty minutes earlier when her patient's IV catheter had dislodged. With an apology, the nurse had awakened her. Amatuzio writes:

> When I sat down wearily on the chair beside his bed, Mr. Stein saw how tired I was and said he was sorry I had to be awakened. But he seemed eager to talk to someone, for he began to tell me how he had died once in the hospital
>
> My heart went out to him as I took his hand. The skin of his left arm was swollen and taut; it was moist and warm, but finding a vein was difficult. I told him that it wasn't his fault that the IV came loose.
>
> "But you're here now," I said.
>
> "Yes," he replied. "I came back to life."
>
> "What happened to you?"
>
> "Blood clots like to form in my legs and travel up to my lungs. The doctors think I have some clots in my legs now. Two years ago, they put a filter, a screen, in my abdomen, in the inferior vena cava, to stop the clots from passing to my lungs. That's when I died."
>
> "I awoke in the post anesthesia recovery room, and the nurses told me that it had gone well."
>
> "Then suddenly," he said, "I left my body, right through the top of my head! I found myself looking down on me—I mean on my body—from the ceiling. I felt so sorry for my body. The doctors and nurses came rushing to my side and began resuscitation.
>
> "I was puzzled because I was just fine. I could feel their concern, and, what's more, I could read their thoughts. I went to the doctor's side and tapped him on the shoulder. He didn't feel me, so I got right in front of him and said, Stop all of that, I'm fine! He didn't hear me, but I could hear every thought he had. One of the nurses was upset that she had to stay and help. I knew her thoughts. She was looking forward to a date right after work!"
>
> "You mean that you could read every thought they had?"

"Yes, it's strange, but it was almost like feeling every thought—like reading their minds!"

"That's incredible."

"I watched them working furiously on my body. They were using shock paddles—my body jumped every time the paddles were used. Then the man in the bed next to me had a cardiac arrest."

"How did you know that?"

"I watched it—the whole thing. His heart stopped pumping and he left his body, too, right through the top of his head. And did he ever look surprised to see me! I communicated with him by just thinking and told him what had happened."

"We watched the confusion below us from some spot up near the ceiling. There was only one emergency cart, and the doctor was shouting orders and calling for help. The shock paddles were on the emergency cart, and the poor doctor would shock one body and then turn around and shock the other. There weren't enough supplies because so much had been used on me."

"So, what did you do?"

"Well, it became clear to us that we couldn't communicate with them, and, you know, it seemed odd, but I didn't feel attached to my body, so we both left the room."

"How did you do that? Did you go through the doors into the hallway? I mean, how did you move?"

"Well, this sounds strange again, but we just thought our way over to the hallway—we didn't go through the doors, we went through the wall. I remember seeing the waiting room near the operating room. There were still several people there, and I could feel their concern for the well-being of their loved ones. Then we moved on."

"To where?"

"We left the building. We went right through the wall. I remember looking back at the red brick and mortar And then we were outside. All was calm and still, but it seemed different, somehow warm, and then I saw it."

"Saw what?"

"Off in the distance I saw—no, I felt—the most amazingly beautiful light. It was so bright; it was made up of every color of the rainbow and more. As we approached this dazzling light, I felt the most incredible joy and awe and sense of grandeur I've ever experienced—words don't do it justice. Then the light opened up into a cone or tunnel. I felt a rush as I moved through it. There were incredible colors there—some I had never seen before or since. I saw my mother and father, my dear aunt, and my dog. They were smiling at me, and it seemed like a joyful reunion, a celebration.

"As I traveled upward toward the source of all this joy, I grew more aware. The brilliant, dazzling colors shimmered, and I began to realize . . . well . . . everything. All at once, I remembered the purpose of my life. I understood how it all worked. I realized that it was all, somehow, perfect. I was overwhelmed and stunned by the loving kindness that surrounded me.

"I was still aware of my companion, who continued to accompany me. Suddenly, I realized—or maybe it became clear—that I could not stay, that I must return to my body. In that instant, I knew with crystal clarity the reasons why. But my companion, the other man who left the recovery room with me, got to go toward that dazzling light."

Mr. Stein was silent as tears streamed down his face. Then he said, "I have never told the entire story to anyone before."

"Thank you for telling me," I replied softly. Then Mr. Stein spoke again.

"The next thing I knew, I was back in my body. Everything hurt. I felt sick and I was tired, and I hurt all over. But I was also amazed—amazed at what had just happened to me. Most of all, I remember the incredible peacefulness. It seemed as though, truly, nothing mattered. I was so overwhelmed that I just kept it all to myself and kept trying to remember all that had happened.

"The next day, my doctor told me what had transpired in the recovery room—that I had had a heart attack and that they had almost lost me. Approximately a month later, at one of my check-up visits, I decided to tell my doctor about this experience. I was still overcome by the immense sense of purpose and peacefulness I now felt. I jumped right in, telling how I had left my body and floated up in the air near the ceiling, how I watched his efforts to resuscitate me.

"He said, 'You must have had an unusual reaction to the anesthetic medication.'

"I replied, 'It was the most real thing that has ever happened to me.'

"'You don't know what you are saying," the doctor responded. "You were dead, dead and gone. We attempted resuscitation for over fifteen minutes. Your heart was not pumping! Then, bang, your heart started again, and here you are. Alive and recovering."

"Doctor," I told him, "I watched you during that incredible resuscitation."

"Impossible—you were unconscious," the doctor asserted.

"Well, I saw that the man in the bed next to me died too, and that you had only one emergency cart and one set of defibrillation paddles, and that there weren't enough medications, and that you moved back and forth between his bed and mine. I felt how worried, frustrated, and concerned you and the staff were."

"You couldn't have known that," the doctor answered. "Someone must have told you. I can't believe this. I don't know what you believe happened, but for all intents and purposes, you were dead."

Mr. Stein told Amatuzio, "We never spoke of that experience again. I felt embarrassed and even doubted it for a while—but I have never forgotten it, and, in my heart, I know that it happened."

"Has this changed your life?" I asked Mr. Stein.

"Oh, yes, in several ways. First, I don't fear death at all. I know that we do not die. The experience called dying that I had was the most magnificent thing that has ever happened to me. Second, I know that love is really all that counts, and that it is of no consequence to store up or value material things. It is who we are that matters. And last, I try to learn something each day—to gather knowledge and then try to apply it to make this world, my world, a better place."

Amatuzio told Mr. Stein that she believed him and thanked him for sharing his incredible story. She realized that she hoped and even dared to believe that what he said was true.

She held this experience with Mr. Stein in her heart "for weeks, months, and years." Remembering that it had changed his life, perhaps it had begun to change her life as well.[16]

Amatuzio, in her 2006 book *Beyond Knowing: Mysteries and Messages of Death and Life from a Forensic Pathologist*, captures another example, that of the near-death experience of her father, who was also a physician. After surgery for a ruptured intestine, when his condition was critical, he had an extraordinary experience that he shared with her.

16 Janis Amatuzio, *Forever Ours: Real Stories of Immortality and Living from a Forensic Pathologist* (New World Library, 2004), 47-54.

"I had fallen asleep," her father began, "in the middle of the afternoon. The nurses had drawn the window shades. Then, I had the sense of leaving that hospital room and traveling across a vast space in what seemed like . . . seconds! I was moving effortlessly, flying."

"I arrived at the most magnificent place I could ever remember. It was green and lush, the colors were so vivid, and there was the most beautiful music I have ever heard. It filled the place. The Light there just glowed, so bright and so gentle. It was so familiar."

Her father then said he came to river where all his family and friends who had died were on the other side. They were happy to see him, but when he began to wade the river, they turned their backs. Then he knew it wasn't his time to join them.

That evening his surgeon, upon examining him, said with an amazed look on his face, "Your intestines are working! You're going to be okay!"

In her book *Beyond Knowing*, Amatuzio also describes an extraordinary experience in the operating room while a patient was undergoing emergency surgery to repair a ruptured blood vessel.

"Minutes passed quickly, then suddenly the cardiac monitor began beeping loudly. His heartbeat had abruptly gone from its regular rhythm into a life-threatening ventricular fibrillation." Then his heart stopped.

"All of a sudden, something happened that I still cannot explain. I saw, or more accurately felt, a shimmer of light in the corner of the room above the foot of the angiography table. I quickly looked to see if the pump team was using a lighting device that perhaps reflected off the wall, but they were not. I looked again, somewhat puzzled, and suddenly had the profound sense of a deep, overwhelming, calm presence, in stark contrast to the frantic activity in the room. It was unmistakable! I was amazed.

"As I stared at the glimmer in the corner of the room, an odd thought formed in my mind, and I clearly heard these words, *He's watching and he's fine!* I didn't know where these words came from and didn't fully understand their significance, but they were manifestly clear."

The surgical team continued resuscitation efforts but were unable to revive him.[17]

17 Janis Amatuzio, *Beyond Knowing: Mysteries and Messages of Death and Life from a Forensic Pathologist* (New World Library, 2006), 167-169, 42 and 47.

Neurosurgeon, Eben Alexander

Eben Alexander had been an academic neurosurgeon for over 25 years, including 15 years at the Brigham & Women's Hospital, Children's Hospital, and Harvard Medical School in Boston. In 2008, he was struck down with acute bacterial meningoencephalitis and spent a week in a coma with what his doctor described as a "markedly altered mental state." When antibiotic treatment was unable to overcome his infection, Alexander's death seemed certain. He did survive, however, and his doctor "confirms that his recovery was 'remarkable'."[18]

On his website Alexander affirms: "My coma taught me many things. First and foremost, near-death experiences and related mystical states of awareness, reveal crucial truths about the nature of existence. Simply dismissing them as hallucinations is convenient for many in the conventional scientific community but only continues to lead them away from the deeper truth these experiences are revealing."

Second, his experience convinced him that: "The conventional reductive materialist (physicalist) model embraced by many in the scientific community, including its assumption that the physical brain creates consciousness and that our human existence is birth-to-death and nothing more, is fundamentally flawed. At its core, that physicalist model intentionally ignores what I believe is the fundament of all existence—consciousness itself."[19]

In his 2021 book entitled *Proof of Heaven: A Neurosurgeon's Journey into the Afterlife*, Alexander describes his near-death experience in detail.

His initial experience during his coma was simply darkness. He didn't know who he was or where he was. When he heard pounding and smelled the decay of death, he began to panic. Soon, however, he saw a swirling shaft of light and followed it up into a living world of bright light and beautiful music.

He discovered that he was flying over a lush countryside. He saw below him streams and fields and people. Then a lovely girl riding on the wing of a butterfly joined him, as beautiful butterflies surrounded and flew beside them.

18 Eben Alexander, *Proof of Heaven: A Neurosurgeon's Journey into the Afterlife* (Simon & Schuster, 2012), 183-184.

19 Eben Alexander, "My Experience in Coma," http://ebenalexander.com/about/my-experience-in-coma/. Accessed July 29, 2024.

Without any spoken words, the girl told him that he was loved, had no need to fear, and could do nothing wrong during his visit in this world. As flocks of transparent orbs crossed the sky above them, she explained that he would learn many things during his visit but would return to his physical life on earth. She communicated to him telepathically, and he was amazed that he clearly understood her.

Hearing and seeing seemed to be a single experience in the reality he was visiting, and he absorbed the flow of information effortlessly. Then he was embraced by a brilliant orb of light, and through the orb, God the Creator revealed to him that there were many universes—all powered by love but also challenged by evil, and all enabling free will choices for conscious beings.

Alexander learned that our human purpose on earth is to become more loving and to discover that our "truest, deepest self is complexly free" and capable of immense compassion. After he regained consciousness, his first words to his family were "all is well."

In *Proof of Heaven* Alexander laments that the worldview of science is opposed to even considering the spiritual reality he experienced. "This other, vastly grander universe," he affirms, "isn't *far away* at all. In fact, it's right here—right where I am, typing this sentence, and right there where you are, reading it. It's not far away physically, but simply exists on a different frequency. It's right here, right now, but we're unaware of it because we are for the most part closed to those frequencies on which it manifests."

Having experienced that life does not end with brain death, Alexander feels he has a duty to share with others what he saw "beyond the body and beyond the earth."[20]

20 Eben Alexander, *Proof of Heaven*, 9-10, 29-32, 38-41, 45-49, 73, 80-81, 84-85, 154-157.

Atheist Scientist, Nancy Rynes

"As a scientist, science writer, and corporate trainer, for over two decades Nancy aligned herself with the skepticism prevalent in so much of the scientific community. She remained an atheist until her life-changing bicycling accident and near-death experience. Now, Nancy is an avid spiritual seeker as well as practitioner of compassion, kindness, contemplative prayer, and present-moment awareness. Drawing on the transformational wisdom learned during her near-death experience, she integrates the teachings of love, compassion, kindness, gratitude, and joy that form the foundation for a peace-filled, meaningful life."[21]

Rynes explains that on January 3, 2014, "while riding my bicycle in town, I was struck broadside by a truck. My injuries were so severe that I am still recovering from some of them. By all accounts of the doctors who treated me, I shouldn't have lived. 'Most people die from injuries like yours,' my surgeon and primary care physician insisted. They were right. I shouldn't have lived. In fact, I came very close to death twice during those first few days. During those brushes with death, I had two near-death experiences that promised to change the way I look at life, the way I experience life, and the way I feel about the concepts of God and Spirit.

"Before we go any further, let me say that I debated about putting this out there, but I realize that it has to be right now. I feel in my heart that it's not good to hold onto this experience. At least one of my friends is soon facing the final transition, and I would hope this post, in some small way, helps her make peace with moving on to the afterlife."

"My first near-death experience happened when the truck initially struck me. In human time, this near-death experience lasted just a few minutes. As I was struck, I realized my consciousness was in two places simultaneously. One part, very scared and animal-like, was firmly inside of my broken body that was stuck on the vehicle's axle and being dragged under the truck. The other part, a very calm, dispassionate observer, hovered out in front of the truck, watching the whole scene unfold from a distance. This dual consciousness seemed quite normal to the observer part of me. The observer was calm about the whole thing, and I remember the feeling that this was all happening for a reason, that there was nothing to fear. The observer: me, watched as witnesses

---

21 Nancy Rynes, https://www.nancyrynes.com/my-story. Accessed March 10, 2021.

stopped, called for help, and as the paramedics arrived. When the paramedics started working on me, my two selves came back together. Once I was stabilized enough to move, they transported me to the nearest trauma hospital. It turned out that my head and spinal injuries were so severe that I needed surgery. My lower spine would need reconstruction, but only after the bleeding in my brain stabilized. In the meantime, the trauma team admitted me to the intensive care unit (ICU). I pondered that initial split-consciousness experience for a few days in the ICU while I awaited surgery. I had no explanation for being in two places at the same time, or for experiencing the accident from two different vantage points at once. In my scientifically trained mind, I didn't know how consciousness could split apart with one part of me traveling outside of the body. Finally, I dismissed it as just an oddity of the crash and almost dying. It wasn't important, and it most certainly wasn't 'real.' Or so I thought.

"Perhaps because the first experience wasn't enough to get me thinking about spiritual matters, three days later during surgery, I was pulled right into the thick of things. I had another near-death experience but this one was different. Instead of simply experiencing events unfold from outside of my body, my consciousness was ultimately brought to a Place unlike anything I have ever experienced. The beauty and utter peace of the Place defies human words. I felt totally calm, loved, and whole. I also felt a deep, profound sense of LOVE permeating everything there. It was big love, as if the structure of this place was somehow made of love. Love was everywhere because there was nowhere that wasn't love. I can't explain it any further than that. I never wanted to leave this Place. One woman greeted me. Although she said it was a form that 'she' took at that time to make it easy for me to relate to her. She was a stranger to me, although I was somehow not a stranger to her. She moved with me throughout the landscape, telling me things that I and the rest of the world needed to remember; things we'd forgotten or perhaps never learned. These things were reminders that would help us live a beautiful life on Earth. She said she was a spokesperson for everyone in Heaven.

"Somehow, she was a conduit for the information I was being given, because if I met and communicated with everyone who wanted to speak with me, I would be overwhelmed. It felt as though we were together for days, even weeks. The amount of information she passed on to me was staggering. I am still processing it. But eventually she insisted it was time for me to go back to my life. The thought of that made me weep like a child. I didn't want to go back. This Place was too beautiful and loving for me to want to leave. But she insisted that I had a life to live. It wasn't time for me to be here for good. I argued up and down and even yelled a few times. Can you imagine, arguing with a Being such as this? But I did. I argued and cried. I insisted I didn't want to go back to a broken body and all the repercussions from this experience that awaited me. She watched me with what I felt was sadness, but she insisted that it was my time to go back. As I opened my mouth to argue again, I was back in the surgical recovery room. I was confused, weeping, and already missing that Place and the Being who I'd met there. No: I am no longer an atheist or agnostic, (although, at this point I don't want to put a label on what I am). I did have the good fortune to be shown Spirit in a way that made me realize that I can no longer deny It for myself. These experiences have opened my heart to all peoples, all faiths, and all beliefs in a way that I would not have thought possible. I will share a small bit of the first thing she taught me. We are primarily here to Love: to practice Love, to show Love, to experience Love. Hate is not the language of Spirit, nor is fear. Love is. It is a Love that has no conditions or strings attached. It is simply Love in all its forms.

"I was asked to share this with as many people as possible, so that is what I intend to do. That's what I promised, after all. I am not sure yet how I will get out the information. I think communicating on a blog is a good start, but I expect that some larger form of publication will be in the works too. Yes, this is all real. No, I didn't make up or embellish any of it. I understand that some of you will think I'm crazy or hallucinating. Some of you may find any explanation to deny my experiences, because they feel uncomfortable to you. Some people I have known for years may choose to distance themselves from me. This could cost me much. I was an agnostic scientist until just a couple of months ago, after all. But this is me and my life now. I trust that telling my story and all that follows will help more than it hurts; that it gives people hope, and that it brings people together. It may be that telling the story brings new people or opportunities into my life as well. All is as it should be. While my time on the Other Side (aka, 'Heaven') was brief in human terms, when I was there it felt as if weeks or months were passing. I observed an amazing amount in, at most, a couple of human hours.

"The first wonderful thing that I experienced was the beauty of Heaven, both visually and in a feeling-sense. When I was there, a landscape of gently rolling hills surrounded me. Flower-filled grassy meadows spread out on the hills around me. There were huge, deciduous trees in full leaf. The trees were larger and grander than any here on Earth and surrounded the meadows. There was the barest sense of a light mist, clinging to the tops of the trees, as if it were a humid, summer morning. The sky showed a very light blue, like what you might see at the ocean's shore, with wispy clouds and a very bright but somewhat diffuse golden light. That was the visual. But there is more to Heaven than what we can see with our eyes. Below the surface visuals was a well of feeling fueled by love, peace, and an abiding Presence that I will call Spirit or God. Through the landscape around me I sensed a profound feeling of peace, brightness, goodness, and love. The Beauty I felt really does deserve a capital B. It wasn't just pleasing to the eye: there was something deeper to it, more harmonious, more blessed, and more powerful.

"Everything felt tied together by love and peace, and the beauty of the scenes around me was the product of this unconditional love. While the beauty of Heaven took my breath away, the sense of love completely ensnared me and made me want to stay there forever. I felt a deep sense of that love flowing through all things around me: the air, the ground below my feet, the trees, the clouds, and me. I felt the love flowing around me, flowing through me, and eventually capturing me by the heart. I felt supported by a loving Presence so powerful, yet so gentle, that I cried again. I had never experienced such unconditional love and acceptance in all my years on the planet."

"Each soul might see the *landscape* differently, but all sensed and *saw* the love that formed the basis for everything in the same way. That love and peace seemed to shimmer as glimmers of light beneath the surface, winking in and out of visual sight. It had colors and sparkle and texture. It seemed to take the form of what I saw, like trees, a meadow, but at the same time it was also separate from the forms themselves. The closest I can come to explaining what Heaven *looked* like to my feeling-senses is to point you to the work of artist Ken Elliott. His paintings come closest to capturing what I felt underlying the landscape Over There."[22]

Her website adds: "Nancy believes that the road to true happiness starts with acting in love and gratitude: loving ourselves for who we truly are, loving others for the Divinity and creativity we each hold inside and showing gratitude for our lives by living our core truths as fully and abundantly as possible. Her 2015 book, *Awakenings from the Light*, dives into these and other topics, giving the reader concrete examples of how to make spiritual wisdom a very real part of life on Earth."[23]

---

22 https://www.nderf.org/Experiences/1nancy_r_ndes.html. Accessed August 2, 2024.
23 Nancy Rynes, "My Story," http://www.nancyrynes.com/. Accessed August 2, 2024.

ICU Physician, Laurin Bellg

ICU physician Laurin Bellg relates the following account in her 2016 book, *Near Death in the ICU: Stories from Patients Near Death and Why We Should Listen to Them.*

> In his eighty-seventh year, Dr. Martin discovered that he had cancer and decided to decline medical intervention.
>
> When I first met Dr. Martin, I had been consulted to help manage his increasing respiratory distress from the metastatic disease that had sprouted from his colon cancer and settled in his lungs. Offering him the respect I felt he was due, I addressed him by his title when I introduced myself. Setting formalities aside he invited me to call him by his first name, but professional graces being what they are, I found that difficult so I just called him Dr. John. Smiling, he reciprocated by calling me Dr. Laurin. We immediately hit it off.
>
> Over the ensuing days, as he grew weaker, his family increased their vigil, maintaining more of a presence in the inpatient hospice where he had recently been transferred. The atmosphere was purposely serene and he looked peaceful. One day, as I dropped by to see him as part of my daily rounds, I was surprised to find him alone. "Where is everyone?" I asked.
>
> "They were too sad and it was bringing me down, so I sent them away," he joked. "No, I told them I needed to rest so they stepped out for lunch."
>
> "Would you like me to come back later?" I offered.
>
> "No, it's fine. Actually, I wanted to talk to you about something."
>
> Finding a chair and pulling it to his bedside, I sat down facing him. He reached out his hand to me and I took it. We sat there for a moment with him looking down at the covers and I could tell he was gathering his thoughts to speak, so I waited for him to break the silence. Finally, squeezing my hand before releasing it, he looked up at me with direct eye contact and I could see his resolve, as if he had decided to entrust me with something very personal.
>
> "I'm not afraid to die, because I've died twice before." Tilting his head slightly and squinting his eyes, he regarded me, weighing my reactions.

In 1944 he was fresh out of medical school when he enlisted to serve in World War II as a field physician. Barely three months into his overseas assignment, while heading out with part of his unit to an outpost triage area for the freshly wounded, their transform jeep was hit by mortar fire, killing the driver and severely wounding the rest of them. Two of his companions died before help could safely transport them back to the hospital, and Dr. John sustained extensive abdominal trauma. Bleeding heavily from his wounds, he passed out on the way back to the Army Hospital they had left barely two hours earlier.

His next conscious memory was that of floating above his body in the operating room, watching as blood rushed in and pooled in the crevices of his open abdomen as quickly as they could clear it away. He knew all of the doctors and nurses as friends and colleagues, and he found it incredibly strange to be watching them in such a detailed manner as they fought intensely to save him.

"I can't find the damn bleeder!" he heard the surgeon say in frustration.

Dr. John heard it all; he saw it at all. He was astonished at how aware he was as he looked. Then a sound distracted him and his attention was drawn to the slowing of his heartbeat on the monitor near his head. At the same time, he felt himself drifting farther away from the drama of the surgery. The last thing he recalled of that scene was the surgeon cursing and yelling out that they were losing him—and his own solitary thought, "I must be dying."

His next awareness found himself completely and peacefully enveloped in what he could only describe as a soft shroud of mist with tiny points of light blinking in and out, as they darted quickly back and forth all around him. He felt completely weightless and peaceful, void of any fear. The feeling of love was immense, almost unbearable, and recalling it now, Dr. John's voice became fragile as he paused to fight back tears.

Retaining his composure, after a few moments he continued. He described floating in such a beautiful and bright place of total peace that he lost all thoughts and concerns related to anything connected to his physical existence. He was aware of nothing except how good it felt to be there where he was—wherever that was. How long he lingered in this space he could not say because time had immediately lost meaning for him.

Suddenly, though, he heard a very distinct voice say gently but firmly, "You can't stay, John. It's not your time to die." Whether the voice was male or female he couldn't determine, but it was commanding and he did not protest. Instinctively, he knew it would be pointless to argue.

Still feeling peaceful and detached, he felt himself descending and slowly his body came back into view as the mist surrounding him dissipated and he could once more hear the clamor and tension of the operating room. Hovering above the scene, he watched the weak representation of his pulse on the monitor slowly gaining strength as the resuscitation efforts of the surgical team reclaimed their hold on Dr. John's physical body.

"Thank God," he heard the surgeon whisper to himself as he stepped back and let an attendant wipe sweat from his brow.

This was Dr. John's last awareness of that particular episode. As he lay drifting in and out of consciousness on the surgical ward—a large, open room lined with several beds along each wall, separated only by curtains—he found his thoughts often drawn to that mysterious event that defied any explanation he could come up with. What he had seen and experienced had been so real. He knew that under the effects of anesthesia, he shouldn't have been able to see his body or the surgical team the way he had. Yet it had been so clear.

He missed the way that weightless space felt, especially when the effects of the morphine wore off. Whenever the racking pain of his surgery washed over him, he longed for the loss of physical sensation he had experienced in *that cloud of total peace*, as he would come to refer to it. But, as Dr. John had suggested when he started telling me about his experience, it would not be the last time he would be there.

As he began to recover and to gain strength, he was started on a clear liquid diet to test the ability of his damaged gut to handle oral intake. While sipping tepid broth from a cup one day, it suddenly went down the wrong way and he began to choke. In the violent paroxysms of coughing that ensued, he popped some of the sutures that held his abdomen together and blood began seeping from his belly, soaking the bandages and leaching onto the sheets beneath him. Frantic calls for help erupted all around him. A nearby surgeon grabbed a gurney and began issuing orders to get him back to the operating room.

That's the last he remembered until he was again in the surgical suite staring down at his body. He watched as a team quickly set up a sterile field and began breaking down the rest of his abdominal sutures. He saw them dive deeper into his belly to reach the repairs from his previous surgery that had broken loose during his intense fit of coughing. Once more, he lost a lot of blood and became very unstable. That's when he died for the second time.

With vital signs losing hold, his body quickly decompensated into an unstable cardiac rhythm that required several minutes of resuscitation to bring him back. He saw the whole thing from above his physical body and watched the team fighting to keep him alive before he drifted away once more into what he referenced as a beautiful space of total love and acceptance.

This time he described the reunion with *the cloud of total peace* as euphoric. It was like coming home after being away for so long. He then slowly became aware of another presence that he could feel but could not necessarily see. He knew he was not alone, but what was strange to him was that the presence seemed so familiar—he knew it intimately and it knew him. He was certain of this without knowing why. Again, the voice told him he must return, that it was not his time to die.

Once more he descended toward his body as the resuscitation efforts succeeded. But this time was different. He felt himself only loosely tied to his physical body as he drifted in and out several times, spontaneously floating above and beside himself on numerous separate occasions. When this happened, he was fully aware of his surroundings and other conversations going on around him, although looking at his body on the bed below, his physical self was sleeping or sedated. He shouldn't have been aware and watching himself, he reasoned, but he was.

Working out for himself that the most logical explanation must be that his medical catastrophes had resulted in some mental imbalance, he decided not to breathe a word of his experience to anyone lest they think him crazy. He had invested too much of his life and energy into becoming a doctor. It was too great a risk to his career to admit that he had perhaps, as he ultimately determined, suffered some type of psychosis. He worried that in talking about his two deaths, as he now referred to them, he would lose credibility and potentially his license to practice medicine.

The experience changed him though—internally at least. The more time that passed and the saner he felt, the less inclined he was to think he was crazy. But the experience fit no process or paradigm he was familiar with. He couldn't explain it to himself, so how could he possibly explain it to others? Not growing up in a particularly religious family, and always a natural pragmatist, he had never even entertained the thought of a life after death or considered the possibility that consciousness could survive beyond the physical body. Yet he had experienced it—twice!

As he lay dying, he confessed to me deep regret about how he had let the thick veneer of our professional code restrict what he shared with others. When his patients had shared personal stories with him of their own near-death encounters, he confessed that even then he was afraid to tell them what had happened to him. Enslaved by a social and professional persona he felt obligated to uphold, as much as he wanted to, he could never muster the courage to share something so personal with his patients. In hindsight, he felt that he had robbed them of the gift of a validation of their experience from someone they looked up to and trusted.

"If I had only had the courage to tell my patients that the same thing has happened to me," he confessed, "I would have done them a great service. But I was too concerned with my own reputation—what my colleagues and patients would think of me. And I have to say," he paused, and then continued quietly, avoiding direct eye contact, "it remains one of the greatest regrets of my life, both professionally and personally.

"Even as my own wife lay dying," he continued softly, "I didn't have the courage to tell her that I believed something wonderful waited for her on the other side. I just couldn't find the words and in her last moments I didn't want her to wonder why I had withheld that from her all those years." Cupping his hands loosely in his lap and with shoulders slumped forward, he lifted his eyes toward me and grinned, "I'm guessing she knows by now, eh?"

"Probably," I affirmed with a smile. We chuckled together.

So I understand Dr. John's reserve—I've lived it. I'm grateful to him, though, for his display of courage in sharing a very personal story with me. Because of his generosity of spirit and words of quiet wisdom, not only as a patient but also as a fellow physician, I found the confidence to document these wonderful stories that patients have graciously allowed me to share with you.[24]

---

24 Laurin Bellg, *Near Death in the ICU: Stories from Patients Near Death and Why We Should Listen to Them* (Sloan Press, 2016), 1-12.

Neurosurgeon, James R. Doty

Doty was a resident surgeon at Walter Reed Hospital when, after a car accident, he was brought into the hospital as a patient requiring emergency abdominal surgery. In his book, *Into the Magic Shop: A Neurosurgeon's Quest to Discover the Mysteries of the Brain and the Secrets of the Heart*, he tells his remarkable story.

When Doty awoke after surgery, he heard the vice chairman of general surgery shouting at the chairman that Doty was bleeding out because the chairman had "missed a bleeder." The chairman at first protested but was persuaded by Doty's rapidly falling blood pressure. As a nurse wheeled Doty back into the operating room she said to him softy, "Stay with us, Jim. We need you."

After being anesthetized again, Doty was in darkness until he found himself up by the ceiling looking down at his pale body and the surgeons searching for a bleeder in his opened abdomen.

Suddenly he was floating along a river, headed toward a bright light. People he had known greeted him from the banks of the river. He saw his father and felt accepted as never before. His mother was in her bathrobe, smiling. His brother was laughing with him in their Lancaster bedroom. He even saw himself putting on a physician's white coat for the first time.

As he came closer to the light, he was embraced by its warmth. Somehow, he knew the light was love, and that love was the only thing that really mattered. He wanted to "be one with all things" in the light.

A prick on his foot brought him back into his body. He opened his eyes, and seeing the nurse who had spoken to him before asked, "Did I die?" She said he hadn't had a cardiac arrest, but the surgeons took four liters of blood out of his belly. And It took sixteen units of blood to restore his blood pressure.

After he fully recovered and did some research, Doty learned that as many as fifteen million Americans have described having a near-death experience with memories similar to his. Their memories often included out-of-body awareness, a life review, seeing or hearing deceased loved ones, experiencing unconditional love, and traveling through a tunnel or on a river toward a light. Similar accounts had been reported in other cultures and historical periods.

For instance, Plato's *Republic* describes a soldier awakening on his funeral pyre twelve days after he seemed to be dead. Doty also read British admiral Beaufort' description of his near drowning in 1795 and American physician A. S. Wiltse's account of nearly dying in 1889 from typhoid fever.

In 1968 Celia Green reviewed four hundred accounts of out-of-body experiences that seemed to confirm consciousness could continue apart from our bodies. In 1975, psychiatrist Raymond Moody published a book about these anomalous reports and identified them as *near-death experiences*.

Doty asserts, however, that "the experiences of the heart" deserve more attention from scientists than possible experiences of consciousness in an afterlife. Why, he asks, do so many travel toward the light and warmth of love? He suggests that near-death experiences reflect the longing of our hearts. "To be loved unconditionally. To be welcomed. To feel the warmth of home and family. To belong."

Doty admits he doesn't know what happened to him when he nearly died during his second surgery. He does know, however, that he has *died many times in this life.*

The lost boy, who he was, died in Ruth's magic shop (a part of his life that I'll explain in a moment). The young man who was ashamed and afraid of his father, but who nonetheless struck him, died the day he left home and went to college. Eventually the arrogant neurosurgeon he became would suffer his own death.

"We can die a thousand times in this lifetime," Doty asserts, "and that is one of the greatest gifts of being alive." The night of his near-death experience what died in him was the belief that Ruth's magic—which she had taught him in her magic shop when he was twelve years old—had made him immune to trauma and failure. At the same time, he let go of his fearful belief that he was alone in the world.

After fully recovering from his near fatal surgery, Doty felt embraced by love. This experience strengthened his trust that "who we are today doesn't have to be who we are tomorrow and that we are connected to everything and everyone."

He realized how far he had come from a summer in Ruth's magic shop. What he didn't know then was how far he had to go. Perhaps seeing Ruth beside the river was a warning that he had not yet understood what she had tried to teach him.

As a twelve-year-old, he'd met Ruth in a magic shop near his home. Doty was just browsing when Ruth began to talk with him. Before he left the shop, she had challenged him to spend an hour Monday through Friday with her for six weeks to learn *real magic*. He did and learned from Ruth how to meditate, relax, and visualize the life goals he wanted to achieve. She also urged him to discover and follow his moral compass, by "opening his heart" to the needs of others.

Doty pursued his goal to become a successful surgeon, and he created a medical tech company that made him wealthy. Just before the stock market crashed, he arranged to donate $75 million of his assets to several charities. After the crash that reduced the value of his investments, his lawyer called to see if he wanted to cancel his donation. Doty said he'd think about it and get back to him.

Ruth had taught him the real magic was "the power of compassion to not only heal each of our own wounds of the heart but the hearts of those around us."

He had learned studying medicine that "the heart sends far more signals to the brain than the brain sends to the heart—and while both the cognitive and emotional systems in the body are intelligent, there are far more neural connections that go from the heart to the brain than the other way around." He also knew it was misleading to identify the mind as rational and the heart as relational, as "ultimately the mind and heart are one unified intelligence."

Doty recalled Ruth telling him that "the wounds of the heart" offer "the greatest opportunity to grow." Closing his eyes and quieting his breathing, he allowed his heart to open . . .

He sent forgiveness to himself for the mistakes he had made. He sent love to his parents for "doing the best they could." He sent love to Ruth, who was the kindest person he had known. He sent love to every child struggling with poverty, or who had addicted parents, or who felt alone and thought it was their fault. He sent love to everyone who had questioned their own worth and to all those who believed that money determined their value in life.

Suddenly, he felt "enveloped by warmth and love—a deep inner peace and an absolute certainty that everything was going to be OK—only this time he wasn't going down a river toward a white light while bleeding out on an operating table."

He called his lawyer and told him to go ahead with the $75 million charitable donation. As he hung up the phone, Doty heard his lawyer say, "Holy shit." Then there was only silence. Doty knew he would continue to have plenty of money. Moreover, he was sure it was time to focus on becoming a person of worth, instead of pursuing wealth. He felt free to follow "the compass" of his heart.

To act on his convictions, Doty founded and is the director of the Center for Compassion and Altruism Research and Education (CCARE) at the Stanford University School of Medicine in Palo Alto, California. He also continues to be a clinical professor of neurosurgery at the Stanford University School of Medicine. He is the former CEO of Accuray (ARAY:NASDAQ) and holds multiple patents. His book, *Into the Magic Shop*, has been translated into 40 languages.[25]

25 James R. Doty, *Into the Magic Shop: A Neurosurgeon's Quest to Discover the Mysteries of the Brain and the Secrets of the Heart* (Avery, 2012), 193-203, 210-233, 272-273 and https://ccare.stanford.edu/people/james-r-doty-md/.

Part II

Research on Spiritual Reality

Psychoanalyst, Elizabeth Lloyd Mayer

Some scientists who haven't had a near-death experience have had extraordinary experiences that altered their lives in ways they are unable to explain scientifically. Elizabeth Lloyd Mayer, a psychoanalyst and professor of clinical psychology, reported some of these stories in her book, *Extraordinary Knowing: Science, Skepticism, and the Inexplicable Power of the Human Mind*, published two years after her death in 2005.

Her publisher, Penguin Random House, explains that Mayer decided to write this book after an astonishing experience challenged her materialistic worldview. In 1991 her daughter's hand-carved and very valuable harp was stolen. When the police were unable to locate it, a friend suggested she consult a dowser who had found many lost objects. With little hope but nothing to lose, she contacted the dowser in Arkansas. Two days later he phoned to say the harp was in a house on a block of a particular street in Oakland, California. Mayer posted "lost" information on telephone poles along this block, and with the help of a neighbor of the man who had taken the harp was able to recover it.[26]

After Mayer had researched several experiences of extraordinary knowing and published an article exploring these remarkable states of consciousness, other scientifically trained professionals began to share with her their unusual experiences.

A physician told her that twenty years earlier he had been diagnosed with bone cancer that would likely be fatal. A marathon runner, he had found relief from despair only while running. After two hours of running one morning, he was suddenly overcome by a sense of light that seemed to be radiating from within his bones. The next week his X-rays were clear. He told his wife he had recovered due to his jogging, but he didn't admit to her that he *knew* the light he saw within his bones in some unknown way destroyed his cancer cells. And he never mentioned his experience to his medical colleagues.

A well-known neurosurgeon who was experiencing terrible headaches came to see Mayer, looking for relief from his pain. Humbly he told her of his remarkable success in performing life-threatening surgeries but then described the recent debilitating headaches threatening his career.

26 https://www.penguinrandomhouse.com/books/109557/extraordinary-knowing-by-elizabeth-lloyd-mayer-phd/. Accessed July 27, 2024.

When Mayer asked if the headaches had affected his teaching of residents who were training in the hospital, he admitted that he had loved teaching but had to stop. After hesitating, he explained to Mayer that he couldn't reveal the secret of his surgical success. When a patient needs surgery, before operating he sits at the patient's bedside, waiting for "a distinctive white light to appear around his patient's head." He only operates if he sees this light, as he has learned from experience that if no light appears the patient will not survive the operation.

When Mayer asked him when his headaches began, he paused before acknowledging that his headaches had begun on the day that he resigned from teaching.

As word spread of her strange research, psychoanalytic and medical colleagues began to tell her more about their anomalous experiences. They'd never shared these with anyone but wanted to tell someone in confidence and chose Mayer. Every story was bizarre and inexplicable.

A physician said that when one of his patient's entered his office, he knew before she said a word that her mother had died. A counselor who was sound asleep awoke because he thought he heard a shot from a gun; in the morning, he learned that at the time he awakened his patient has used a gun and tried to kill herself.

Another physician suddenly felt that the son of her partner was seriously injured. When she phoned her partner, he sent a text to the son's roommate and soon received back a text confirming that his son had been in a terrible car accident. The partner arrived at the hospital in time to help decide about the surgery that saved his life.

Still another colleague was riding a bus and smelled the perfume that the ex-wife of his brother used to wear. At the next stop, she got on the bus.

Mayer kept notes, read reports, and eventually wrote her book. Excerpts from *Extraordinary Knowing* on the topics of intuition, healing, and visions are included in later sections of this book.[27]

---

27 Elizabeth Lloyd Mayer, *Extraordinary Knowing: Science, Skepticism, and the Inexplicable Powers of the Human Mind* (Bantam Books, 2007), 1-11.

Cardiologist, Pim van Lommel

In 1986 Dutch cardiologist Pim van Lommel began studying the near-death experiences of patients who survived cardiac arrest. In 2001 *The Lancet,* a prestigious medical journal, published a review of the research by van Lommel and his colleagues. In 2007 van Lommel published in Dutch a book which in 2010 was released in English with the title *Consciousness Beyond Life: The Science of the Near-Death Experience*. This book has been republished in China, France, Germany, Hungary, Italy, Latvia, Poland, and Russia.[28]

In 2011 the *Annals of the N.Y. Academy of Sciences* published an article by van Lommel entitled "Near-Death Experiences: The Experience of the Self as Real and Not as an Illusion." In 2013 the *Journal of Consciousness Studies* published his essay entitled "Non-local Consciousness: A Concept Based on Scientific Research on Near-Death Experiences During Cardiac Arrest."

In the *Annals* article, van Lommel reported that cardiac arrest survivors have experienced perceptions from outside their bodies while their brains had no measurable EEG activity. Many of these memories have been objectively confirmed by doctors or nurses. "In a review of 93 corroborated reports of potentially verifiable out-of-body perceptions during a near-death experience, about 90% were found to be completely accurate."[29]

Van Lommel personally verified a near-death recovery in a coronary care unit, which was also observed and then recorded by the attending nurse. The ambulance crew had brought into the emergency room a comatose man. Once in the hospital, he was given artificial respiration with a mask and heart massage defibrillation. To intubate the patient, van Lommel had to remove the dentures in his mouth, which were placed in a drawer of the crash cart. After about ninety minutes of intensive resuscitation efforts, the patient's heart was beating regularly and his blood pressure was near normal. Yet, he remained unconscious and was transferred to an intensive care unit.

When van Lommel next saw the patient, he was wide awake and immediately asked for his dentures. He recalled seeing that van Lommel had removed them and put them in the crash cart drawer. The patient described other details

28 Pim van Lommel, https://pimvanlommel.nl/en/pim-van-lommel/biography/. Accessed July 29, 2024.

29 Pim van Lommel, "Near-Death Experiences: The Experience of the Self as Real and Not as an Illusion," *Annals N.Y. Academy of Sciences*, 2011, ISSN 0077-8923, 22-23.

of the room in which he had been intubated while unconscious. The patient also told van Lommel that he had been afraid they were going to stop trying to resuscitate him. Further, he added that his experience had removed his fear of death.[30]

Van Lommel explains in the *Annals* article what near-death experience researchers mean by a life review: "Patients survey their whole life in one glance; time and space do not seem to exist during such an experience. Instantaneously, they are where they concentrate upon, and they can talk for hours about the content of the life review even though the resuscitation only took minutes. This panoramic review of one's life seems to contain all the conscious and unconscious aspects or the essence of oneself in constant and instantaneous connection with the consciousness of others."

One of his patients recalls that not only did he see everything from his own perspective, but he also knew what everyone involved in the event was feeling and thinking. He saw how his actions had influenced others and felt regret for mistreating them.

In the *Annals* review van Lommel notes that cardiac arrest survivors often recall meeting deceased relatives or friends during their near-death experiences. "If deceased acquaintances or relatives are encountered in an otherworldly dimension, they are usually recognized by their appearance, and communication is possible through what is experienced as thought transfer."

One cardiac arrest survivor remembers: "I saw, apart from my deceased grandmother, a man who had looked at me lovingly, but whom I did not know. More than 10 years later, at my mother's deathbed, she confessed to me that I had been born out of an extramarital relationship, my father being a Jewish man who had been deported and killed during the Second World War." When his mother showed him a picture of his biological father, he recognized him as the unknown man he had seen during his near-death experience.

Van Lommel and his colleagues verified, in interviews eight years after the near-death experiences of their patients, that the lives of their patients had been fundamentally altered by their experiences. They also found that the processes of transformation that had begun in people had intensified after eight years. Near-death survivors continued to feel the unconditional love that had transformed their lives.[31]

---

30 Pim van Lommel, *Consciousness Beyond Life: The Science of the Near-Death Experience* (HarperOne, 2010), 20-21.

31 Pim van Lommel, *Annals*, 19-23.

Consciousness, van Lommel asserts, "is not visible, not tangible, not perceptible, not measurable, and not verifiable." Without consciousness, however, "there is no perception, no thought, no feeling, no knowledge, and no memory."[32] Every experience of reality is filtered through our conscious experience.

To account for conscious experiences during near-death experiences, van Lommel suggests that our endless and enhanced consciousness "with all the aspects or essence of self finds its origin in, and is stored in a nonlocal space, as wave fields of information." And that "the brain only serves as a relay station for parts of these wave fields of consciousness to be received into or as our waking consciousness or ego in the shape of measurable and changing electromagnetic fields."

He affirms in the *Journal of Consciousness Studies*: "One cannot avoid the conclusion that endless or nonlocal consciousness has always existed and will always exist independently from the body, because there is no beginning, nor will there ever be, an end to our consciousness. There is a kind of biological basis of our waking consciousness or ego, because, during life, our physical body functions as an interface or place of resonance. But there is no biological basis for our whole, endless, or enhanced consciousness because it is rooted in a nonlocal space. Our nonlocal consciousness with the experience of self does not reside in our brain and is not limited to our brain. So our brain seems to have a facilitating, and not a producing, function to experience consciousness."[33]

On his website van Lommel, in three clear sentences, summarizes what he has learned from his decades of research: "The near-death experience is an authentic experience which cannot be attributed to imagination, psychosis, or oxygen deprivation. After such a profound experience, patient's personalities underwent a permanent change. In Van Lommel's opinion, the current views on the relationship between the brain and consciousness held by most physicians, philosophers, and psychologists is too narrow for a proper understanding of the near-death experience phenomenon."[34]

---

32 Pim van Lommel, *Consciousness Beyond Life*, 285.

33 Pim van Lommel, *Journal of Consciousness Studies*, 20, Ni. 1-2, 2013, 39. The phrase "resides not our brain" was replaced by "does not reside in our brain."

34 Pim van Lommel, https://pimvanlommel.nl/en/. Accessed July 29, 2024.

Coauthors, Peter and Elizabeth Fenwick

Peter Fenwick is a neurophysiologist and neuropsychiatrist in the United Kingdom. He and his wife Elizabeth published *The Truth in the Light: An Investigation of Over 300 Near-Death Experiences* (White Crow Books, 2012).

Peter Fenwick explains in the Introduction that the experiences described in it are responses sent to him or David Lorimer, chairman of the International Association of Near Death Studies (UK), by those who learned of their interest through a television program, radio broadcast or magazine or newspaper article. He and Lorimer asked 500 of those who contacted them to answer a detailed questionnaire about their near-death experiences. More than 350 replied, and *The Truth in the Light* considers and comments on these responses.

Of those responding, 78% were women; 80% were older than 18 at the time of their experience, while 9% were ten or younger. About half were Anglicans, 12% Roman Catholic, 19% were members of other Christian denominations, and 1% were Jewish. 8% identified as agnostic and 2% as atheist. Few of those who identified as religious regularly attended religious services. Only 2% had been aware of near-death experiences before they had one.

How had the experience affected them? 82% said they have less fear of death, and 48% believed in life after death. 42% shared that they were more spiritual as a result, 22% claimed to be a "better person," and 40% said they were more concerned about social justice. 47% thought they had become more sensitive.[35]

After reviewing these responses, the Fenwicks were certain that most, if not all, reported near-death experiences represent real experiences, not some form of fabrication. Most of those having such an experience were reluctant to talk about it, fearing ridicule. If it hadn't really happened, these people would never have dreamed of claiming it had. Here are a few excepts from *The Truth in the Light.*

"I remember going into a tunnel," M. Hilton reports. "At the end of it was a very bright light. I heard beautiful music, something I'd never heard before. I saw people standing around, all being happy with one another."

35 Peter and Elizabeth Fenwick, *The Truth in the Light: An Investigation of Over 300 Near-Death Experiences* (White Crow Books, 2012), 1-3.

Mrs. Mary Lowther remembers, "I seemed to *float* along a corridor towards, then into, all-enveloping brightness and light, with indefinable shades of pastel-like colors. There were what I can only describe as billions of beautiful shimmering forms, no outlines, and they were all *cloaked* in what looked like a garment of translucent light."

Many survey respondents wrote that warmth seemed to emanate from the light they saw. Mrs. Holyoake, encountering Christ, could feel this warmth. Dawn Gillot, too, recalls a beautiful and warm light.

David Verdegaal remembered that he saw a light that seemed to grow brighter until its brilliance embraced him. He felt loved like a child. Whether he lived or died, he knew God would be with him.

Allan Pring, an ex-RAF pilot, assumed he had died during surgery when he *woke* and felt he was floating in a vast empty space. Then he had a life review beginning with his childhood, which included some experiences he regretted. He had not, however, felt judged... except by himself.

Mrs. G. U. Dunn found herself in a lane with high, golden gates. Beyond the gates there was a beautiful garden with flowers of every kind. She pushed the gates and tried to enter but could not get in.

Mrs. Joan Hensley wrote of her experience that she is now less frightened of dying and has come to believe there is life after death. She also has faith in God, but thinks God cares more about love than being religious.

Anne Thomson believed she could no longer cope with three small children and one dreadful husband (whom she later divorced), so she took a massive overdose of sleeping tablets that nearly killed her. During her near-death experience she felt drawn toward a spiritual light but was pulled back into her body. The experience, however, led her to believe that God had saved her and would help her raise her children.[36]

Researchers have suggested, the Fenwicks write, that few hellish experiences have been reported because they are quickly forgotten. Yet, the Fenwicks' research does not substantiate this claim. They did learn that frightening experiences were experienced by some as encouragement to make better choices in life.[37]

Truth in the Light verifies that near-death experiences create memories when the brains of those having the experience are offline, which challenges the scientific view that our minds depend on our brains. Might our minds be

36 Ibid., 59 77, 88-90, 115, 129, 134.
37 Ibid., 195-196.

separate from our brains and available to form memories when we are unconscious? William James in his book *Human Immortality* (1898) suggests that there is a transcendent reality beyond the brain, and that our brain and mind are linked and exchange information.[38] Van Lommel makes a similar proposal based on his research, which identifies our minds as nonlocal and endless, and our brains as facilitating our minds.

Publications by Peter and Elizabeth Fenwick include *Past Lives: An Investigation into Reincarnation Memories* (2001), *The Art of Dying (2008), The Truth in the Light: An Investigation of Over 300 Near-Death Experiences* (2012), and *The Hidden Door: Understanding and Controlling Dreams* (2020).

38 Ibid., 259-260.

Shared Death Experiences

Psychiatrist and near-death researcher Raymond Moody reports in his 2016 book, *Glimpses of Eternity: Sharing a Loved One's Passage from this Life to the Next*, on "shared death experiences" involving physicians, nurses, and other professionals providing care for patients in hospitals and hospice environments. These shared experiences involve extraordinary knowing by healthy and often scientifically trained persons.

Moody describes this experience related to him by a psychologist in North Carolina. "The deathbed scene is not fully in this world. And although I am not religious, hospice work has awakened me to a spiritual dimension of life. In my opinion, everyone who works with the dying long enough must have some awareness of these experiences. I believe the spiritual experiences of dying people somehow leak out and pervade the area around them. If you step into that area with the right temperament, you will receive, I feel, a sense of the sacred in the presence of the dying.

"The bedside of the dying offers a view into eternity. Like looking through a window into elsewhere, from time to time I see lights and twice have had clear views of what appear to be structures. On both occasions I saw patients leave their bodies in a cloud form. I saw them rise out of their bodies and head toward these structures. I would describe these clouds as a sort of mist that forms around the head or chest. There seems to be some kind of electricity to it, like an electrical disturbance. I don't know if I see it with my physical eyes, but it's there all the same. There is no doubt in my mind that you can sometimes see people depart for the other side."[39]

Physician Denise Jean Jamieson, on the faculty of the Medical College of Georgia, had been staying with her ill mother, when her mother stopped breathing. Jamieson gave her dying mother CPR for about thirty minutes, until she accepted that continued resuscitation was futile.

Suddenly Jamieson felt she was leaving her body and saw her mother also hovering beside her. Light was streaming into the room through a portal and deceased friends of her mother were entering the room. After her mother greet-

39 Raymond Moody and Paul Perry, *Glimpses of Eternity: An Investigation into Shared Death Experiences* (Rider, 2010), 102-03.

ed them, they all left through the portal which closed "like a camera lens."[40] Jamieson was surprised to experience her mother's departure but as a physician is surely a credible witness to what occurred.

Pediatrician Melvin Morse, in his 1994 book *Parting Visions: Uses and Meanings of Pre-Death, Psychic, and Spiritual Experiences*, reports on many shared death experiences that he documented in his practice and his research. For instance, he shares this sad but striking experience of the mother of a newborn boy named Jason:

She was reading in her living room while her baby was asleep, when she felt someone else was in the room. When she looked up, she saw her father who had been dead for a year. He said to her, "Jason is coming with me." She knew then that her baby would soon die, and a week later he did. Describing her experience as a dream doesn't alter the fact that what she learned about her son was objectively confirmed by his death.[41]

Moody reminds us that although a dying person may be impaired by declining physical or mental capacities or pain medication, those sharing in a death experience as caregivers or loving relatives are *not*. Therefore, the experiences of caregivers and relatives can't be dismissed as merely subjective and emotional fantasies.

Moody reports the shared experience of his family when his mother died. As he held hands with his wife, his two sisters, and their husbands, Moody saw the light in the room change "to a soft and fuzzy texture." And the joy as their mother's spirit passed on.[42]

In his 1993 book *Reunions: Visionary Encounters with Departed Loved Ones*, Moody explains that in ancient Greece three hundred *sanctuaries* were created in memory of Asklepios, a highly respected physician.

Pilgrims seeking healing came to the sanctuaries and stayed until they had a dream of Asklepios who invited them to enter the central room. Those hoping to be healed lay on narrow beds that slightly elevated their heads. Our modern word for clinic is derived from the Greek word, *klinis*, for these temple healing beds.

---

40 Ibid., 7-8.

41 Melvin Morse and Paul Perry, *Parting Visions: Uses and Meanings of Pre-Death, Psychic, and Spiritual Experiences* (Villard Books 1994), 66, 17-18, 54-55, 50-51.

42 Raymond Moody, *Glimpses*, 49-50.

The Greeks believed that Asklepios came into the sanctuary at night and healed pilgrims while they slept. Grateful for their healing, some hired stonecutters to inscribe their visions on the pillars in the sanctuary.[43]

Moody, while pondering how to help bereaved families who longed to see their deceased loved ones, made an unexpected discovery. In a bookstore, as he was browsing in the psychology section, he inadvertently knocked off the shelf a book entitled *Crystal Gazing*, which was published in 1900. The author, Northcote Thomas (1868-1936), describes the practice in ancient cultures, known as *scrying*, of communicating with the dead by gazing into crystals, mirrors, or pools of water.

To study mirror-gazing by contemporary individuals, Moody created a quiet and darkened environment with a mirror positioned so subjects gazing into it would not see themselves. He invited his psychology students to participate, but soon faculty and many others also asked to take part.

By 1993 when he published his book, *Reunions: Visionary Encounters with Departed Loved Ones*, more than 300 volunteers had sought a "facilitated apparition" experience and half had reported "complex communications" either during their time in the apparition room or soon after.[44] By 2012 and after several hundred more apparition experiences, Moody reported that more than 80 percent "saw departed loved ones."[45]

Moody also includes in *Reunions* his own surprising experience of communicating with his deceased paternal grandmother. Moody writes:

"I want to emphasize how completely natural this meeting was. She was there in front of me, and as startling as that fact was, I just accepted it and continued to talk with her.

"I did hear her voice clearly, the only difference being that there was a crisp, electric quality to it that seemed clearer and louder than her voice before she died. Others who'd had this experience before me [in similar apparitional reunions] described it as telepathic or 'mind to mind' communication. Mine was similar. Although most of my conversation was through the spoken word, from time to time I was immediately aware of what she was thinking, and I could tell that the same was true for her.

"She appeared no different from any other person except that she was surrounded by what appeared to be a light or an indentation in space, as if she were somehow set off or recessed from the rest of her physical surroundings.

---

43 Raymond Moody and Paul Perry, *Reunions: Visionary Encounters with Departed Loved Ones* (Villard Books, 1994), 16-18.

44 Ibid., 112.

45 Raymond Moody, *Paranormal*, 226.

"As a veteran of altered states of consciousness, I can say that my visionary reunion with my grandmother was completely coherent with the ordinary waking reality I have experienced all my life. If I were to discount this encounter as hallucinatory, I would be almost obliged to discount the rest of my life as hallucinatory too."[46]

All 'afterlife' evidence will inevitably involve subjective experience, for this kind of experience necessarily involves someone who is alive communicating with someone who is dead. Also, those who are dead cannot be objectively known as material beings, for being 'alive' in an afterlife no longer requires a physical body. Yet, conversations and communication can be remembered, witnessed, and recorded.

Each afterlife experience is unique, but this is also true of every past event. Perhaps our best standard for evaluating afterlife evidence would be the legal standard for a court of law. A judge or jury in the courtroom considers both subjective testimony and objective facts, as a reasonable person should, by assessing the coherence of all the evidence and also the credibility of witnesses. Isn't this the standard we should apply when asked to verify *afterlife* experiences?

Moody concludes his 2012 book, P*aranormal: My Life in Pursuit of the Afterlife*, by recalling his response to an interviewer's question, 'What do you think happens when we die?'

He writes: "My mind flashed back to the thousands of people I have listened to over the years as they told their story of near-death and the miraculous journey when they almost died. I thought about my own journey to the brink of death. I realized that, yes, I was very experienced in both objective and subjective research into life after death.

"What do I think happens when we die?" Moody replied, "I think we enter into another state of existence or another state of consciousness that is so extraordinarily different from the reality we have here in the physical world that the language we have is not yet adequate to describe this other state of existence or consciousness. Based on what I have heard from thousands of people, we enter into a realm of joy, light, peace, and love in which we discover that the process of knowledge does not stop when we die. Instead, the process of learning and development goes on for eternity."[47]

Death in many cultures has been recognized as a departure of the soul from the body. The word soul, however, has at least two meanings. *The Encarta World English Dictionary* defines the soul first as: "The complex of human at-

---

46 Raymond Moody, *Reunions*, 26-29.
47 Raymond Moody, *Paranormal*, 245.

tributes that manifests as consciousness, thought, feeling, and will, regarded as distinct from the physical body." The Dictionary also offers a second definition of the soul: "In some systems of religious belief, the spiritual part of a human being that is believed to continue to exist after the body dies."

In Plato's *Phaedo*, Socrates refers to death as a "separation of the soul from the body," and the book *Studies in Greek Philosophy* asserts that Socrates used the phrase "care of the soul" to refer to the study of the afterlife.[48]

Psychiatrist Raymond Moody in his 2023 book entitled *Proof of Life After Life* documents evidence of the soul in shared death experiences reported to him. Experiences not only involving a dying patient, but also experiences that are "shared" with someone who is healthy and has medical training. He mentions the experience of Dr. Jamieson, a member of the faculty of the Medical College of Georgia, which was reported earlier in this chapter. After her mother's death, Jamieson saw "her" leave her body and join deceased loved ones who had come to lead her "home."

In *Proof of Life After Life*, Moody also reports on shared death experiences that include a physician, nurse, or other medically trained caregiver seeing a mist leave the body of a dying person as well as changes of the light in the room. At the beginning of this chapter, I quoted a psychologist who told Moody he twice saw "patients leave their bodies in a cloud form." He further described these "clouds" as a "mist" over or around their heads.

Moody notes in *Proof of Life After Life* that Louisa May Alcott, who was present with her family's physician, Dr. Christian Geist, when her sister Elizabeth died, wrote in her diary that she and Dr. Geist saw "a light mist rise from the body" of her sister and "vanish in the air."[49] A contemporary physician reported to Moody that while visiting a patient who died suddenly, "a mist rose from her body" that was "pinkish and hovered like a cloud."[50]

In Spokane, Washington, a newspaper published the question: "Does anyone really know when the human spirit or soul departs from its physical body?" A registered nurse named Karen responded by sharing that after her patient died, she saw a "pink mist" above his body. She also felt "an odd change

48 Raymond Moody Jr. and Paul Perry, *Proof of Life After Life, 2. Gregory Vlastos, Studies in Greek Philosophy*, vol. 2 (Princeton University Press, 1995), 8.

49 Raymond Moody, *Proof*, 4. Louisa May Alcott, *Her Life, Letters, and Journals*, ed. Ednah Dow Littlehale Cheney (Little, Brown, and Company, 1919), 97-98.

50 Raymond Moody, *Proof*, 134.

in the quality of light in the room." Karen acknowledged that there is no "scientific proof" of the soul, but said she felt she had "witnessed" the soul of her patient leaving his body.[51]

Moody reports that many doctors and nurses have shared their "supernatural experiences" when caring for dying patients. For example, a nurse told him that while caring for her dying mother, she saw a "powerful white light" that was "glorious." Also, the nurse caring for Swiss psychiatrist Carl Gustav Jung, who recounted his near-death experience in his autobiography, told Jung that she saw a bright light surrounding him.[52]

Moody explains that often in the room of a dying person medical caregivers see a light with no apparent source, which fades after the death of the patient. Those present usually describe the light as beautiful or brilliant. One caregiver explained, "There is something transitional going with the spirit, the mind as well, that it isn't just the physical."[53] Amatuzio in her book *Beyond Knowing* describes her experience of such a light.

Veteran surgeon Jeff O'Driscoll reports entering the surgical theater and at once sensing "a divine presence." Then seeing a light above the patient, which he says he "knew innately" was the "eternal soul" of the patient's wife killed in the same accident that nearly killed her husband.[54]

Moody notes that researchers Peter Fenwick and Sue Brayne, report that more than 25 percent of doctors, nurses, and other hospice carers describe seeing light around their patients. On the basis of his sixty years of reviewing evidence of near-death experiences, Moody asserts that: "Our consciousness persists in another framework of reality after our physical bodies die."[55]

---

51 Ibid., 135-136. Catherine Johnston and Rebecca Nappi, "EndNotes: A Nurse's Tale: The Spirit Leaves the Body," Spokesman-Review, July 12, 2012, https://www.spokesman.com/blogs/endnotes/2012/jul/12/nurses-tale-spirit-leaves-body.

52 Ibid., 129. Carl Gustav Jung, *Memories, Dreams, Reflections* (Vintage Books, 1989), 289.

53 Ibid., 146. Peter Fenwick, Hilary Lovelace, and Sue Brayne, "Comfort for the Dying: Five Year Retrospective and One Year Prospective Studies of End of Life Experiences," *Archives of Gerontology and Geriatrics* 51, no. 2 (September-October 2010): 4, https://a.edu/22946305/Comfort_for_the_dying_five_year_retrospective_and_one_year_prospective_studies_of_end_of_life_experiences.

54 Ibid., 139. Jeff Olsen and Jeff O'Driscoll, "Their Shared Near-Death Experience Formed an Unbreakable Bond," *Guideposts,* https://guideposts.org/amgels-and-miracles/life-after-death/their-shared-near-death-experience-formed-an-unbreakable-bond; and an interview with Paul Perry in 1999.

55 Ibid., 176.

Jeffrey Long, NDERF Research

In 1998, radiation oncologist Jeffrey Long created the Near Death Experience Research Foundation (NDERF) to collect with surveys the data that would facilitate studying the elements of near-death experiences.

In this chapter I share insights from two published reports on the research completed by the NDERF: Long's 2011 book *Evidence of the Afterlife: The Science of Near-Death Experience* and his 2016 book *God and the Afterlife: The Groundbreaking New Evidence for God and Near-Death Experience.*

Evidence of the Afterlife reports on more than one thousand surveys completed on the NDERF.org website. Long evaluated these responses by applying the scientific principle: "What is real is consistently seen among many different observations." He argues that this is the legal *reasonable person* standard applied in courtrooms to assess witness testimony, which is inherently subjective.

Long explains that he considered individuals to be near-death if they would die unless their condition improved. Their experience had to occur near death and had to be a lucid memory.

After reviewing the NDERF survey results and the literature on near-death experiences, Long accepts that near-death experiences may include all, but more often some, of these twelve elements.

1. **Out-of-body experiences:** Of the thousand surveyed, 613 experienced separating from their body.

2. **Heightened senses:** 74% felt they were more conscious and alert than normal.

3. **Intense and generally positive emotions or feelings:** 76% had these feelings and half felt "incredible joy."

4. **Passing into or through a tunnel:**_Only one-third of those who surveyed said they had.

5. **Encountering a mystical or brilliant light:** Almost two-thirds saw a light. One wrote "the light still touches me with awe and tears come immediately."

6. **Encountering other beings, deceased relatives or friends:** More than half did. One saw her grandmother who had died when she was a baby as well as other deceased relatives.

7. A sense of alternation of time and space: 60% had no "sense of time" during their experience.

8. Life review: 22% had this experience. Long notes that many respondents experienced empathy as they felt the impact of their actions on others.

9. Encountering unworldly ("heavenly") realms: 40% described beautiful landscapes and flowers or wondrous music and luminous colors.

10. Encountering or learning special knowledge: 56% said they did but many were unable to recall the details.

11. Encountering a boundary or barrier: 31% had. Most realized that if they crossed the barrier, they would be unable to return to their lives on earth.

12. A return to the body, either voluntary or involuntary: 58% affirmed that they had a choice.[56]

In *Evidence of the Afterlife*, Long responds to these questions.

Are near-death experiences possible for patients under general anesthesia? Long reports that psychiatrist Bruce Greyson has verified this unexpected fact. He cites 127 confirmed experiences out of 578 cases.[57]

What are the long-term consequences of a near-death experience? Many survivors reported being healed during their near-death experiences. A man with a deformed hand due to cerebral palsy, after his near-death experience was able to use his hand. This healing was verified by his health-care team.

God and the Afterlife considers NDERF reports concerning God.

All the near-death survivors answered the NDERF survey question, "During your experience, did you encounter any specific information/awareness that God or a supreme being either does (or does not) exist?"

Of 420 experiences in the most recent NDERF survey before 2016, 191 said they had, 62 were uncertain, and 167 said they hadn't.

---

56 Jeffrey Long and Paul Perry, *Evidence of the Afterlife: The Science of Near-Death Experiences* (HarperOne, 2010), 1-18.

57 Jeffrey Long and Paul Perry, *God and the Afterlife: The Groundbreaking New Evidence for God and Near-Death Experience* (HarperOne, 2016), 79-80, 175.

Before their near-death experience, 39% of those responding to this survey thought that God "definitely exists." Two decades after their experience, when they were completing the survey, 72% of the survivors affirmed the existence of God.

Encounters with Love

58% of the survivors responding to the survey said they had felt love or forgiveness or God's unconditional love

God and Light

In near-death experiences, God is often experienced as a bright and loving light. Here are two comments made on the NDERF survey.

"I became aware that I am the light also. We are all part of the light."

"The light knows everything that I've ever done and will do but loves me unconditionally."

God's Appearance

One near-death survivor shared this description.

"All That Is, can be perceived as a force and a consciousness that exists within each individual consciousness and yet is separate from each being or consciousness. It might be called God, but the ideas of god we have are a pale and incomplete shadow of the All That Is that I perceived. We project an idea of a god or gods upon that infinite, creative consciousness, which limits our understanding of the All That Is, in ways that reflect the limited comprehension we have of ourselves and the physical universe."[58]

Purpose, Meaning, and Relationships

Here are two responses on surveys by near-death survivors.

"I learned I hate most in others those qualities that I have in myself but can't see. Love was the key to everything—acceptance and love."

"To overcome our fears, we need to love and accept ourselves and each other. The actions and choices we make can either be from love or fear—love is golden light, fear is darkness."

Heaven

Long notes that most encounters with God occur in beautiful realms that have earthly characteristics but also more intense colors or unusual music. Some survivors report large cities, beautiful buildings, forums, schools, or temples.

---

58 Ibid., 98, 119, 136-146, 151-153, 157-164.

Here is a near-death memory of one NDERF responder.

"Words are inadequate to describe Heaven. But I knew I was home. I knew this was where I'd come from. The grass and trees and flowers were all so exquisite, and a vibration of love flowed back to me from them. I heard music, more melodic and beautiful than anyone could write on this earth, just suddenly playing and filling my soul with joy."

Hell

Long points out that among the reports of near-death survivors, there are few experiences that describe hell. He also reports that frightening experiences can lead to positive changes in life. Moreover, he has never read a report of a near-death experience that describes God as sending a soul into a hellish place forever.

Long ends his book *God and the Afterlife* with a personal affirmation of hope. He reports that those responding to NDERF surveys include persons from different countries and varied occupations, including business managers, homemakers, nurses, physicians, educators, pastors, students, and young children.

As a scientist, Long finds this "not only statistically remarkable, but hopeful. In the investigation of the largest collection of near-death experiences to date, we see overwhelming evidence of God. This opens a door for science, for humanity, and for religion. Near-death experiences reveal that death is not an end, but an opening to a wonderful afterlife. I believe this is profoundly good news for all of us."[59]

59 Ibid., 193-196.

Psychiatrist Researcher, Bruce Greyson

In his 2021 book *After: A Doctor Explores What Near-Death Experiences Reveal about Life and Beyond*, psychiatrist Bruce Greyson reflects on more than four decades of research and personal interviews with individuals about their near-death experiences.

Greyson has been on the medical school faculty at the University of Michigan, where he directed the emergency psychiatry service; at the University of Connecticut, where he was Clinical Chief of Psychiatry; and at the University of Virginia, where he held the endowed Chester F. Carlson Professorship of Psychiatry and Neurobehavioral Sciences. He has received numerous research grants from federal agencies, pharmaceutical companies, and nonprofit research foundations.

He has also served on grant review boards, has planned workshops at the National Institutes of Health, and has addressed a symposium on consciousness at the UN. He has received awards for medical research and was elected a Distinguished Life Fellow of the American Psychiatric Association. During his career to date, Greyson has published more than a hundred articles in medical journals that are peer-reviewed.[60]

As a scientist, Greyson asserts there is sufficient evidence to affirm that near-death experiences are caused by a physiological process yet to be identified. He also argues it is possible that near-death experiences are a spiritual gift, due to a nonphysical dimension of reality. Neither of these proposals, however, is a scientific conclusion, as no evidence can disprove either. Greyson suggests both are plausible explanations that could be true without any contradiction.

He also affirms that his research data and personal experience verify that "near-death experiences are quite real and quite profound in their impact and are in fact important sources of spiritual growth and insight—whatever their source."[61]

The scientific challenge for Greyson has been clarifying what is actual evidence for *being real*. Scientists understand many aspects of the physical world, but they also have nonphysical experiences such as feelings and ideas. While

60 Greyson notes: "All of my peer-reviewed journal articles can be downloaded from the University of Virginia Division of Perceptual Studies website at www.uvadops.org."

61 Bruce Greyson, *After: A Doctor Explores What Near-Death Experiences Reveal about Life and Beyond* (St. Martin's Essentials, 2021), 8-12.

nonphysical experiences can't be studied directly, in the ways that physical events can, our experiences can be studied indirectly by observing how they affect our physical actions.[62]

Greyson's scientific approach includes historical research as well as personal interviews. He didn't believe claims that persons experiencing near-death had accelerated brain activity, until he discovered the 1892 report on the near-death experiences of mountain climbers written by Swiss geology professor Albert von St. Gallen Heim and published by the *Swiss Alpine Club.*

Heim had had a near-death experience two decades earlier, when he had fallen sixty-six feet down a mountain. Heim was amazed by his experience and located thirty other climbers with comparable stories. Heim reported that his thoughts sped up as he was falling: "What I felt in five to ten seconds could not be described in ten times that length of time." Nonetheless, his thoughts were coherent. His article confirmed that other climbers who had fallen had similar experiences.

Greyson reports that among all those who shared their near-death experiences with him, three-quarters recalled a change in time and more than half reported a feeling of timelessness.[63]

A quarter of those included in his research also experienced a life review. Some saw their entire life pass by, from birth to the present or in reverse order. Others were able to select memories. Most described their life review as far more vivid than any of their ordinary memories. Three-fourths felt their life review had given them a new perspective on their lives. Half experienced some judgment in their life review, which was mostly self-criticism. More than half saw past actions they had taken not only from their own perspective, but also felt the emotions of others who were affected by those actions.[64]

Claude, a seventy-two-year-old farmer, was one of the 116 patients Greyson interviewed who had a heart attack. When Greyson asked Claude what he remembered, he said he'd felt dizzy in the barn and sat down on a bale of hay. Later he woke up in the hospital. Greyson asked Claude if he recalled anything before waking. Claude replied that he thought he was going to meet his Maker, but his pa who had been dead for fifteen years stopped him and said he had to go back and take care of the farm.[65]

From a scientific perspective personal experiences such as Claude's are not objective evidence, and many scientists assert that such anecdotal accounts

62 Ibid., 21-22.
63 Ibid., 30-33.
64 Ibid., 37-40.
65 Ibid., 45-46.

have no scientific value. Greyson argues, however, that most research begins with scientists reporting and comparing anecdotes until patterns become apparent. Then these patterns are formulated into hypotheses that can be tested scientifically.

Many of Greyson's colleagues dismiss near-death experiences as simply fantasy. Greyson's response is that what makes an investigation scientific is not the topic, but whether the study reflects rigorous observations, evidence that can be evaluated, and clear reasoning. For instance, researcher Jan Holden reviewed ninety-three cases of out-of-body perceptions during near-death experiences and proved that 92% were verified by outside sources as completely accurate. These anecdotal accounts, after being verified, became objective evidence.[66]

In 2002 Greyson began to interview people he had interviewed years earlier to see if the memories of their near-death experience had faded or otherwise changed. His interviews confirmed that there were *no* differences between their memories from the 1980s and what they recalled decades later. Based on this evidence, Greyson concluded that studying memories of past near-death experiences is as valid as studying recent experiences.

Greyson reports that 71% of all the near-death experiencers he studied feel the memories of their near-death experiences were—and remain more—vivid than memories of other events. Greyson's research also verifies that memories of near-death experiences feel *more real* than events that most of us would agree *are* real events. Memories of near-death experiences are more intense and include more details than most memories of real events.

Greyson confirms extensive clinical experience and research that have established a decrease of brain activity within six to seven seconds of the heart stopping. After no more than twenty seconds, the electro-encephalogram (EEG) goes flat, as there is no measurable activity in the area of the brain that supports consciousness.[67]

Greyson has found no evidence that decreased oxygen in the brain might cause near-death experiences. Patients experiencing decreased oxygen are agitated and fearful. Near-death experiences, however, are generally peaceful and inspiring. Moreover, oxygen levels measured in those having a medical crisis are lower, whereas oxygen levels measured during near-death experiences are higher.

A multinational research team analyzed language usage in 625 reports of near-death experiences and compared these results to thousands of unusual ex-

---

66 Ibid., 61, 90, 93.

67 Ibid., 93-94, 96, 107-108.

periences reported by people taking any of 166 different drugs. The researchers learned that taking the drug ketamine led to experiences that were similar to near-death experiences, however the side-effects of taking ketamine have not been confirmed in near-death experiences.[68]

Some scientists have argued that near-death experiences might be related to levels of adrenaline, glutamate, serotonin, and vasopressin, all of which transmit signals between nerve cells. There is no research, however, that confirms any such a relationship. Greyson doesn't expect researchers will explore this issue, as altered levels of these chemicals in the brain quickly dissipate making measurements hard to replicate.[69]

Greyson reminds us that the association between the mind and the brain is a fact, but the belief that the brain *creates* the mind is not a scientific fact. He cites examples that illustrate this distinction.

At the age of eight, Steve Luiting nearly drowned. Later as an adult, he told Greyson that while drowning he experienced a radical change in perspective. Initially he was terrified but quickly found himself calmly observing his own drowning. As his child's brain shut down, he felt his mind was able to see his situation more objectively. The experience led Luiting to conclude that our brains filter out most of our experiences and limit the perception of our minds.

Michele Brown-Ramirez at age seventeen hit her head while diving into a swimming pool. When interviewed by Greyson, she described how, while underwater, she felt time go faster and slower at the same time, until it felt timeless. As she felt her awareness being pulled away from her body, she realized she was dying. In that timeless moment, however, instead of fear she felt loved and at peace. She said to Greyson, "I felt free from my brain. And the 'thinking' I had was very free, simple, and clear."

Greyson proposes that these near-death experiences and many others are evidence that our minds—the part of us experiencing consciousness—are not the same as our brains.[70]

As French philosopher Henri Bergson (1859-1941) suggested, "The brain maintains consciousness fixed on the world in which we live; it is the organ of attention to life." Our brains receive thoughts from our minds and focus on those important for survival, converting these thoughts into electrical and chemical signals our bodies can process.

---

68 Charlotte Martial, Héléna Cassol, Vanessa Charland-Verville, et al., "Neurochemical Models of Near-Death Experiences: A Large-Scale Study Based on the Semantic Similarity of Written Reports," *Consciousness and Cognition* 69 (2019), 52-69.

69 Greyson, *After*, 109-110.

70 Ibid., 116-122.

It is obvious, however, that our minds have many thoughts unrelated to our survival. This may be why some who have survived near-death experiences feel disappointed by the reactivation of their brains after resuscitation. As she was riding her bike, Lynn was hit by a car. While unconscious, she had a near-death experience. In her interview later with Greyson, she remembered opening her eyes and thinking, "Shit! All I have is a human brain."

Greyson reports that neurological imaging studies of individuals who have taken psychedelic drugs verify that their mystical experiences are accompanied by a *decrease* in brain activity. He explains that this decrease in activity might reduce the brain's filtering activity and facilitate mystical experiences. In fact, many spiritual traditions use reduced breathing, fasting, or sensory deprivation to induce a state of mind that is more amenable to mystical experiences.[71]

Greyson reports that three-fourths of those who participated in his research said their afterlife experience was blissful with no suffering. They experienced the afterlife as "outside of time" and suggested that earthly time did not exist in the afterlife. Two-thirds continued to have their own feelings and thoughts about what happened but agreed that they had grown spiritually.

Over half of those with near-death experiences said they had a life review and learned from it that all of us must confront what we have done in our physical lives. Almost half said that the afterlife allows observations of the living and even communicating with them. They also recalled having physical-like sensations in the afterlife, such as hearing and seeing, and that in their experience of the afterlife they continued to feel emotions.

Two-thirds said that in their near-death experience they saw or sensed the presence of a deceased loved one. Greyson adds that almost 90% of those he interviewed also said they encountered some kind of divine or godlike being in their near-death experience. Of those, the majority did not know who this being was, yet they felt loved and "at home." Greyson suggests this undermines the claim that near-death experiences simply reflect a person's religious heritage or upbringing. Perhaps, in part, a near-death experience also reflects our increasingly secular experience.

Most experiencers, Grayson reports, say that following their near-death experiences they have felt the presence of *something* sacred in their lives. Among those he interviewed, more than four out of five affirmed an increased faith in a higher power as well as an inner awareness of that power.

---

71 Ibid., 124-129.

During his research Greyson realized he could scientifically study "the experiencers' reaction to meeting a divine being" by evaluating the impact of this experience on their lives.[72]

Among the those participating in his research, 86% said after their near-death experience they were less afraid of death. Also, Greyson says, every study has verified that near-death experiences inhibit thoughts of suicide.[73] Several researchers, he reports, have verified consistent changes in experiencers' relationships to others and in their attitude toward life. Many discovered a new purpose in living.

Greyson compared persons who had nearly died but did not have a near-death experience with those who had near-death experiences. He used standardized questionnaires that measure satisfaction with life, connection to something greater, and a sense of purpose. Results showed that near-death experiencers were "more satisfied with life, more open to positive new directions in life, had more positive changes in relationships with other people, felt more personal strength, had greater appreciation for life, and felt they had undergone greater spiritual growth as a result of their near-death experiences." Also, many said that since their near-death experiences, they had looked for ways of growing spiritually.

Greyson affirms that he found *spiritual growth* most striking in those who were materialistic before their near-death experiences. Of the experiencers he studied, one-third changed jobs and three-fourths significantly altered their way of life.

Joe Geraci, a policeman who almost bled to death after surgery, describes how his life was transformed by his experience. He had been a tough cop but after his near-death experience he was repelled by violence, whether on television or on the street. When his new attitude kept him from firing his gun, and consequently endangering his partner, Joe quit the police force and became a teacher.

When Mickey collected money for the Mafia, he had no sympathy for those who couldn't pay. After communicating with a divine being and a beloved deceased brother during his near-death experience, Mickey left the Mafia. He explained to Greyson that before he sometimes hurt people to make them pay, but after his near-death experience he couldn't do that.[74]

Greyson was surprised to find that some experiencers were angry that they hadn't died. Cecilia, a sixty-one-year-old teacher, had a near-death experience

72 Ibid., 131, 152, 155, 159, 161-162.
73 Ibid., 164-168.
74 Ibid., 186-189.

during surgery for a ruptured appendix. She felt ready to die and became depressed as she began to recover. In a journal she began to express her anger, and in the first entry she criticized God.

Some near-death experiencers remain troubled and create challenges for their families. When he was a teenager, Kenny was electrocuted by a high-voltage power line. During his near-death experience, he had hellish visions but awoke feeling called by Christ to aid others. His parents asked Greyson for help, as Kenny's friends rejected the "new" Kenny. When Greyson included Kenny in a support group, Kenny brought his parents, who continued to attend even after Kenny had left the group.

Greyson ends his book where he began. He suggests that near-death experiences involve both the physical brain and the non-physical mind. He concludes, however, that neither perspective by itself provides a complete description of the near-death experience.

He thinks it is plausible that chemical or electrical activity in the brain at death may cause the mind to separate from the body. Greyson also thinks there "is no inherent conflict between a physical and a non-physical understanding of near-death experiences." He proposes that "the physical and the nonphysical are different levels of explanation."[75]

"I don't know," he acknowledges, "whether some kind of continued consciousness after death is the best explanation for near-death experiences in which experiencers see deceased loved ones, whose deaths were unknown to the experiencer at the time of the near-death experience." He acknowledges, however, that he does not have an alternative explanation for this astonishing but objectively verified fact.

Greyson has confirmed that for many, the most meaningful change after a near-death experience is an increase in their sense of spirituality. He suggests what they mean by spirituality is "the aspect of their personal lives that includes something beyond the usual senses, and a personal search for inspiration, meaning, and purpose, a quest to connect with something greater than themselves."

For many near-death experiencers, this includes the conviction that having loved and cared for others during their lives will be valued the most when they each have their life review in the afterlife.

---

75 Ibid., 194-195, 199-200, 209-211.

Finally, Greyson speaks directly to the readers of *After*, expressing the "hope that your reflections on my words will not end when you put this book down but may continue to live on in your thoughts and feelings about life, death, and beyond."[76]

76 Ibid., 220-223.

Hospice Physician, Christopher Kerr

Christopher Kerr summarizes his experience as a hospice physician in his 2020 book entitled *Death is But a Dream: Finding Hope and Meaning at Life's End.* His co-author, Carine Mardorossian, an English professor at the University of Buffalo, is a friend who keeps her horse in Kerr's barn. While grooming horses together and talking about death and dying, Kerr realized that her interest in his research, as well as her English skills, would be an asset for his book.

The research presented in the book was conducted by staff members at Hospice and Palliative Care Buffalo, including a biochemist, social scientists, doctors, and nurses. Kerr has an undergraduate degree in Psychology, a Doctorate of Medicine, and a PhD in Neurobiology. At *https://www.drchristopher-kerr.com/* he provides updates on his research, writing, and speaking engagements.

Kerr reports that having sat at the bedside of thousands of dying patients, he realized that his view of dying and death had changed. More often than not, as they face death and experience bodily pain, they told him of their wondrous dreams and visions. Patients describe these experiences as "more real than real," and many have told Kerr that these spiritual experiences have overcome their fear of dying.

Kerr notes that religious and sacred traditions have long described dreams and visions prior to death that provide assurance of continuing life. Yet, dying in a modern hospital is not an environment that has welcomed these experiences. Kerr admits, "Our current medical model reflects a limited view of the totality of the dying experience."[77]

Physicians have been quick to dismiss the extraordinary dreams and visions of patients nearing death as delusions, either due to diminished mental capacity or to the drugs administered to patients. Kerr's research, however, enables caregivers to distinguish experiences that result in confusion and fear from those that evoke a sense of acceptance and peace as death approaches.

More than 80% of the patients studied reported at least one "end-of-life" experience prior to their death. 72% of those who saw deceased friends and relatives confirmed that these were soothing experiences. Dying patients clearly distinguished "normal dreams" from these visions. Whether they were asleep

77 Christopher Kerr and Carine Mardorossian, *Death is But a Dream: Finding Hope and Meaning at Life's End*, (Penguin Publishing, 2020), 3-7.

or awake, they insisted these end-of-life experiences were more meaningful and spiritually inspiring than any of the normal dreams they had previously had.[78]

Kerr writes, "Our patients demonstrate again and again what the dying process is truly about—the resurrection of our deepest bonds and the reaffirmation of love, both given and received. Through their end-of-life experiences, those dying often reestablish ties with the people who mattered most to them. In these moments, even patients with fragmented and broken lives find their way to connection and belonging."

To give one example, Joan and her husband Sonny were both dying, but Sonny died first. It was two months before Joan died, but she reported to Kerr that she had visions of Sonny every day until her own death.[79]

Kerr reminds us that dying is not just a physical event. "Near death, the boundaries between the experiential and the spiritual, the body and the mind, present and past, conscious and unconscious impulses, seem to dissolve to provide a sense of transcendence to a place of blissful comfort and serenity."

At Hospice Buffalo, medical staff collaborate with chaplains and religious representatives who visit patients. Kerr writes, "The spiritual and the physical go hand in hand, especially when we seek to ease our patients' transition to their final home."[80]

Kerr says he has witnessed many times "the quiet process of peaceful surrender and well-being," which he describes as "the version of grace and spirituality that takes my patients over the threshold of pain and suffering." Crucial in this transition are the end-of-life dreams and visions, which Kerr explains "are spiritual in the manner in which they alter perception and in the sense of well-being they provide."

"They are spiritual because of the deeply personal process of renewal they trigger in the most secret corners of the self. They are spiritual insofar as they free us from fear and pain and connect us to each other."[81]

---

78 Ibid., 49, 51, and 71.

79 Ibid., 95 and 134.

80 Ibid., 215-218.

81 Ibid., 220-221.

Part III

Extraordinary Knowing

Near-death experiences are extraordinary, in part because the person feels that they are dying or even have died. Researchers have noted that many survivors choose the word "spiritual" to characterize why their near-death experience has been life-transforming. There are, however, numerous reports of extraordinary knowing by persons who describe their experiences in other ways. In this section I explore some of these experiences where people identify these moments of extraordinary knowing as intuitions, healings, visions, dreams, and mystical experiences.

Do these extraordinary experiences verify a kind of conscious knowing that cannot be explained by current scientific models of reality? Might this evidence meet the courtroom standard for judging the testimony of witnesses as convincing, if reasonable and coherent? This standard recognizes that all those experiencing and perceiving an event will recall only partially what might have been more fully recorded by video and sound recording equipment, had it been in place at the time of the event. Also, observers would be selectively interpreting their perceptions on the basis of their awareness of what preceded the event in question and the consequences that are likely to occur after. In the courtroom, evidence is presented by testimony from those who saw or heard or otherwise have knowledge that might enable a jury to construct a cogent interpretation of the event being considered.

The jury's decision after deliberation reflects the understanding of most or all of its members, but the decision is not an objective explanation of the event. That is impossible. I suggest, however, that scientific striving for objectivity is more like the courtroom process than many scientists acknowledge. Pursuing scientific knowledge involves combining objective facts and measurements with more subjective observations and experiences that require interpretation and evaluation, as is the case for a jury weighing evidence in the courtroom.[82]

82 For an entire book of legal evidence, see Victor Zammit and Wendy Zammit, *A Lawyer Presents the Evidence for the Afterlife* (White Crow Books, 2013).

As we consider intuition, healing, visions, dreams, mediums, and mystical experiences, we may discover that these have informed inquiring scientists about the extraordinary reality we understand only in part.

Intuition

Scientists often refer to *intuition* when describing experiences of knowing that can't be explained as the result of their own reasoning process. The French scientist Henri Poincaré (1854-1921) contrasts reasoning and intuition: "It is by logic that we prove, but by intuition that we discover." German physicist Max Planck (1858-1947) said: "Science does not mean an idle resting upon a body of certain knowledge; it means unresting endeavor and continually progressing development toward an end which the poetic intuition may apprehend, but which the intellect can never fully grasp."

Albert Einstein (1879-1955) affirmed that: "I believe in intuition and inspiration. Imagination is more important than knowledge. For knowledge is limited, whereas imagination embraces the entire world, stimulating progress, giving birth to evolution. It is, strictly speaking, a real factor in scientific research." And on another occasion, Einstein asserted: "All great achievements in science start from intuitive knowledge, namely, in axioms, from which deductions are then made."

Philosopher of science Karl Popper (1902-1994) wrote: "My view of the matter, for what it is worth, is that there is no such thing as a logical method of having new ideas, or a logical reconstruction of this process. My view may be expressed by saying that every discovery contains an 'irrational element,' or 'a creative intuition.'"

The highly successful inventor, Thomas Edison (1847-1931), explains: "It has been just so in all my inventions. The first step is an intuition—and comes with a burst, then difficulties arise."[83] Steve Jobs (1955-2011), founder of Apple, declared *that*: "You have to trust in something. Your gut, destiny, life, karma, whatever." He left no doubt that he trusted in intuition. "Intuition is a very powerful thing," Jobs said, "more powerful than intellect." He added, "This approach has never let me down, and it has made all the difference in my life."[84]

83 "Intuition Quotes," *Today in Science History*, https://todayinsci.com/Quotations Categories/I_Cat/Intuition-Quotations.htm. Accessed March 23, 2021.

84 Ruth Umoh, "Steve Jobs and Albert Einstein both attributed their extraordinary success to this personality trait," CNBC: *MakeIt*, Jan.29, 2017, https://www.cnbc.com/2017/06/29/steve-jobs-and-albert-einstein-both-attributed-their-extraordinary-success-to-this-personality-trait.html.

I suggest that many scientists acknowledge the significance of intuition because they think of intuitions as arising from the unconscious level of their own minds. I think most would agree with Edison that intuition "comes with a burst" into consciousness and with Popper that intuition is "creative" from the depths of their own minds.

Isaac Asimov (1920-1992), who was famous for his prolific writing but was also a professor of biochemistry, described intuition as more complex: "How often people speak of art and science as though they were two entirely different things, with no interconnection. An artist is emotional, they think, and uses only his intuition; he sees all at once and has no need of reason. A scientist is cold, they think, and uses only his reason; he argues carefully step by step and needs no imagination. That is all wrong. The true artist is quite rational as well as imaginative and knows what he is doing; if he does not, his art suffers. The true scientist is quite imaginative as well as rational, and sometimes leaps to solutions where reason can follow only slowly; if he does not, his science suffers."[85]

Given these acknowledgements by scientists for the intuitive form of extraordinary knowing, we might assume that intuitive knowledge—although not explained by science—would be highly regarded among scientists. Yet, as psychiatrist Elizabeth Mayer reports in her 2008 book *Extraordinary Knowing*, this is not the case. Her research revealed that scientists who had extraordinary experiences, which could not be explained within the current materialist paradigm of science, kept these experiences secret to protect their professional reputations.

For instance, Mayer writes of a patient named Grace who was a statistician. Grace confided to Mayer that she knew things intuitively which she couldn't have known in any other way. For example, in her third year as a PhD student she had a fellowship and was doing well. Then in a seminar, after her professor gave his students a difficult problem to work out, Grace suddenly knew the answer to four decimal places and blurted it out. The professor responded by accusing her of stealing his notes and refused to continue working with her on her PhD. She had to transfer to another university to complete her dissertation; and in her career she had to conceal her ability to know when an experiment would fail or when a data analysis was wrong. The truth simply came to her without any reasoning that would explain how she knew it.

Grace traced her extraordinary intuition back to her childhood experience of protecting herself and her younger sister from attacks by her father. Late in the afternoon, she would *listen* intuitively for him while she knew he was

85 "Intuition Quotes."

driving home from work. She always knew when her father was drunk. If he was, she would take her sister with her into the closet, so her father wouldn't see them and hit them.[86]

Grace couldn't explain her intuitions, nor could Mayer explain the intuitive knowing shared with her by other scientists. To research intuition, Mayer chose to interview four professional *intuitives* who are well known for being credible. She first phoned Deborah Mangus and asked her to describe her intuitive state of mind.

Mayer reports that Deb said she wasn't sure how she knew what she knew. An image would just appear. With Mayer, Deb saw the word sprite and felt it referred to Mayer's youngest daughter. Mayer was reminded that her neighbor had recently described this daughter as a "real flower sprite." Also, her daughter's fourth-grade teacher had once described this child as like a can of Sprite suddenly opened after being shaken. Because Mayer's daughter often burst into laughter, in class or elsewhere, Mayer's family had nicknamed her Sprite.

When Mayor asked Deb how she started knowing things intuitively, Deb described her childhood experience with her mother. When the phone rang, her mother would tell Deborah it was her Aunt Rosie, and when Deborah answered invariably it was Aunt Rosie. This would happen even when Aunt Rosie hadn't called her mother for months.

Deb told Mayer that she took intuitive communication for granted until she was in first grade. Then when she answered what she thought her teacher was saying, she often found she was replying instead to what Deb *knew* her teacher was thinking.

For different reasons than Grace, Deb too learned to anticipate danger. Her intuitive knowing was useful when she later became a nurse, as she was able to identify problems before confirming them scientifically.

Mayer also interviewed a second intuitive, Ellen Tadd. In their first conversation Mayer gave Ellen only her name before asking Ellen to tell her what she saw. Ellen began by looking at Mayer's right hand, which she said activated her clairvoyance, and then started to describe Mayor's past lives.

She told Mayer, who didn't believe in past lives, to just think of what she was describing as metaphorical. Ellen said she uses past lives to see how the past is affecting a person's present life.

Ellen then shifted her focus to Mayer's children, suggesting that there was some imbalance between her and one of them. Ellen felt the child, who she thought was a daughter, was struggling to overcome a traumatic failure in a

86 Elizabeth Lloyd Mayer, *Extraordinary Knowing*, 10-15 and 97-100.

previous life. Ellen saw her as being extremely serious for her age and suggested Mayer was not helping her daughter by suggesting her decisions were simply casual choices without serious consequences.

Mayer recognized the description of her daughter but remained unconvinced that this was due to an unresolved problem in a previous life until Ellen provided a more detailed description. Ellen said she saw Mayer's daughter in a past life as a Scottish feudal lord who felt guilty for failing to protect his people. One night a group of Picts attacked them, raping the women, torturing the men, and killing everyone still alive. Ellen said Mayer's daughter blamed herself for failing to keep her people safe.

Ellen suggested that when Mayer's daughter asked whether she should color the leaves in a drawing dark or light green, her question really reflected this repressed memory. Mayer's reassurance that either color would be fine didn't recognize that the color choice was a metaphor for a life and death decision.

Mayer was amazed that Ellen had portrayed her daughter's anxiety so accurately, using a past life metaphor. Mayer had recognized that she wasn't helping to reduce her daughter's anxiety but hadn't realized how much was at stake emotionally. Mayer was grateful for Ellen's intuitive insight and was astonished that Ellen was able to assess her relationship to her daughter without ever meeting either of them.

In a second conversation with Ellen, Mayer asked her to consider five names of colleagues that Mayer was considering as possible collaborators in a research project. Ellen quickly described the likely character traits of four of the persons on Mayer's list, and her comments were consistent with what Mayer knew of these individuals. Ellen was unable, however, to locate any information on the fifth person. When Mayer later called the phone number she had for him, she learned that he had died two weeks before she asked Ellen to find and describe him.

Ellen explained to Mayer that as a child she had often known that what people were saying was not what they were feeling. She had slept with a light on because otherwise she saw faces and felt unsafe. He father didn't understand her intuitive experience, but when she was nineteen her deceased mother came to her and not only confirmed her gift but encouraged her to develop it.

Mayer's third interview was with John Huddleston, who had been in private practice as an intuitive for three decades. During this conversation by phone, John recalled how he became aware as a child of his intuitive nature. Around the age of nine, he was in school reading a book about ancient civilizations. As he looked at a "low angle shot" of the Egyptian pyramids, he felt "light-headed, almost to the point of passing out."

This "otherworldly shimmer of experience" was not only fascinating but was revealing to him a level of reality unknown to most people. John was influenced by his mother's artistic practice of waiting to *hear* what the landscape said to her before she began to paint it. He also told Mayer that his grandfather, who had been a professor and writer, went to Walden Pond in 1893 so he could read Thoreau at night by candlelight and sense his spirit. His grandfather also wrote verses about "past life glimpses."

John explained to Mayer that he has a "relaxed focus" when he's communicating with a client. He sees the person's life as a "moving, transforming mural: the client's health, relationships, family, joys and challenges, future—they're all there. So, discerning what's important among all that is essential." John also told Mayer that he thinks many children experience a "luminous world, which includes imaginary playmates, conversations with God, and glimpses of past lives." Most, however, quickly learn that paying attention to their intuitive experiences is not rewarded by their parents or teachers.

Mayer was surprised when John described critically a close family member of Mayer's. Mayer told him he was wrong about the man, but John stood by his statement. Twelve days later Mayer learned that John's intuitive assessment was accurate.

Mayer concluded her research on intuitive individuals by interviewing Helen Palmer, who was well known for her books and workshops. When Mayer phoned Helen and introduced herself only by name, Helen responded by identifying her as a writer who was struggling with a project. Before Mayer told her anything about what she was writing, Helen made several suggestions to improve it. Mayer found Helen's insights extremely helpful and published the much-improved article two months later.

Helen thought that most intuitive "reading" involved becoming empty enough to discern what was entering her mind from outside. She does this by following her breathing until both thoughts and feelings subside. Then she creates an image of whatever she is trying to focus on. She waits quietly, renewing her focus on this image as it wavers, until her intuitive awareness is clarified.

She believes this process of "focused imagination" links everyday consciousness with a "greater reality." When reading another person, she explains, "you know them from the inside" because you are no longer separate. You not only know their thoughts but also experience a more expansive reality.[87]

What has Mayer's research revealed about intuition? Two of these individuals described childhood experiences that were threatening. All four seemed to have had an innate ability that they chose to develop. Each, however, had a

87 Ibid., 43-55.

different way of *reading* a person. Mayer verified that despite their different intuitive methods, each accurately described her life, family, or writing in a way that rationally seems inexplicable.

Healing

Psychologist Jeanne Achterberg (1942-2012) in *Imagery in Healing: Shamanism and Modern Medicine* describes the history of healing in the West, beginning with the Greek philosopher and healer Asclepius (Asklepios in Greek). "The legend of Asclepius was merged with that of the Egyptian god of healing, Imhotep, and with the god Serapis of the Ptolemies. Historians say, 'Apparently the legend was so persuasive, and Asclepius so satisfied the need for a personal, compassionate divinity, that he inherited, replaced, or merged with the power and influences of each local healing god, wherever the Asclepian rites were introduced.' The legend was even incorporated by Christianity, with Saints Damian and Cosmas carrying on the healing traditions."

More than two hundred healing temples, called *Asclepia*, were built in what today are the countries of Greece, Italy, and Turkey. All who came seeking healing were accepted regardless of their ability to pay for the costs of their care. "The diagnosis and healing took place during that special state of consciousness immediately prior to sleep, when images come forth automatically like frames of thought projected on a movie screen. (This is now called *hypnogogic sleep*). During this sensitive, susceptible time, Asclepius purportedly would then appear as a handsome, gentle, and strong healer, who either cured or advised treatment."

Achterberg explains that Aristotle, Hippocrates, and also Galen studied the Asclepian tradition of medicine, and each of them valued the role that the imagination played. Aristotle believed emotions necessarily involve images, which affect the proper function of our organs.[88] Health was understood as both mental and physical; healing involved evoking images in the mind as well using natural anesthetics.

In Europe and the British Isles between 500 and 1300 CE, the imagery for healing rituals involved local as well as Roman and Greek deities. Moreover, Achterberg asserts: "It was the wise women who used the nonrational intuitive aspects of the mind in a healing capacity."

Historian Matilda J. Gage writes that despite persecution by Christian leaders in the Middle Ages, "The superior learning of witches was recognized in the widely extended belief of their ability to work miracles. The witch was

88 Jeanne Achterberg, *Imagery in Healing: Shamanism and Modern Medicine* (New Science Library, 1985), 54-56.

in reality the profoundest thinker, the most advanced scientist of those ages." Witches were *scientific* in the sense that through trial and error they knew what worked. Achterberg suggests that: "much cure must have relied upon the effect of the rituals and incantations upon the imagination, and not the ingredients of the potions."[89] The witches are best understood as imaginative healers.

In England in 1518, the Royal College of Physicians was established to limit the practice of medicine to men who were trained by existing male physicians. Women were excluded. Of course, women in need of assistance in giving birth and treating the illnesses of their children continued to find midwives and other wise women. Yet, Achterberg asserts, historians estimate that in Europe and the British Isles "a few hundred thousand to nine million women were murdered between the years 1500 and 1650," after being accused of practicing medicine.

"It was not purely 'femaleness' that was so blatantly challenged with regard to the role of women in science and medicine. It was, rather, that the qualities traditionally associated with women posed a threat to what was eventually to become known as the Newtonian world view, i.e., the concept that the body, as well as the universe, was a great machine. Intuition, feelings, nonrational thought, holism, nurturance, and the imagination have scant place in the thought mode of a universe made of cogs and wheels." Achterberg asserts: "The ostracism of the shamanic aspect of women's medicine, at first economic and political in nature, later became necessary because science could not account for what appeared to be transpersonal phenomena."[90]

Note the difference, however, between the statements about intuition in the previous chapter by scientists, and how Achterberg is using the word. All the quotes praising intuitive knowing in the previous chapter came from male scientists. This is not surprising as until the twentieth century almost all scientists were men. These scientists acknowledged that intuition is irrational yet praised its imaginative character as the source of their creativity. They were not challenging a mechanistic view of the world but were only pointing out how new insights in a mechanistic, natural world actually appeared in *their* minds, from an unconscious source. They were praising themselves—their creative if unconscious selves—for intuitive impulses they experienced and then rationalized.

In contrast, Achterberg describes women healers as experiencing and evoking shared images that their patients could experience as healing. Often these women healers were midwives helping women give birth and care for their

89 Ibid., 58-60. See M. J. Gage, *Women, Church and State* (Chicago, 1893).
90 Ibid., 67-71.

children. They were not physicians claiming to know the reason for physical suffering but were relying on herbs and words that had a history of relieving suffering. These intuitive and creative women were mediating the unknown natural forces and energies that transcend mechanistic models of medicine. Their healings were not the result of individual intuitions but instead were due to skillful transpersonal mediation using imagery.

The neurosurgeon, interviewed by Mayer, who waits for the assurance of a white light around the head of his patients before operating did not describe his extraordinary knowing as intuition. Perhaps this is because unlike the scientists praising their intuitions, he was not experiencing a "burst" of personal insight. His extraordinary knowing came in some way from his patients, or at least was communicated through them. He recognized that his experience ensuring the success of his surgical intervention in the life of a patient was *not* coming from his own unconscious mind.

Mayer also reports an extraordinary healing shared with her by Dr. Robert Pyles, who at the time was president elect of the American Psychoanalytic Association.

Pyles had been "diagnosed with a viral meningoencephalitis." The physicians treating him also found a large mass in his chest "with the infiltrate" in his lungs, which "turned out to be disseminated sarcoidosis." Pyles lost forty-five pounds as the disease invading other organs. Primarily to calm himself, he started meditating and running. He had young children and yet appeared to be facing an early death.

As he ran, he began to focus his mind on the lesions in the cells of his body. He felt himself "becoming those cells and those lesions." He was astonished to discover that the lesions began shrinking. He ran and he watched the lesions resolving, feeling that *he was them resolving*.

The mass decreased in size and after three years the infiltrate was gone. Eventually, the mass also disappeared. His recovery was completely inexplicable from the "traditional" medical perspective and was described in a journal as a "spontaneous resolution of a disseminated sarcoidosis."

Pyles remains convinced that his running created a state of mind that enabled him to heal his cells and lesions by "becoming them." This experience not only saved his life but led him to recognize that medicine has little understanding of the power of our minds to heal our bodies.[91]

91 Elizabeth Lloyd Mayer, *Extraordinary Knowing*, 1-9.

To protect his career, Pyles concealed this knowledge from his colleagues and only revealed it privately to Mayer for her research about extraordinary knowing. Although his recovery was not actually spontaneous, Pyles allowed the medical journal to report that it was.

Biophysicist Joyce Whiteley Hawkes responded differently to her extraordinary experience by leaving her career as a cell researcher and becoming a meditative cell-level healer. Combining her scientific knowledge with training from Chinese and indigenous healers, Hawkes discovered through meditation how to reach the cells in our bodies with energy that enables cell healing.[92]

In her 2006 book, *Cell-Level Healing: The Bridge from Soul to Cell*, Hawkes explains she soon learned that individuals with a regular meditative practice were more likely to respond to whatever energy flow she could provide. Those without any meditative background were less likely to improve their health.

Hawkes learned from her first teacher that there was an energy flow in our bodies, which naturally keeps us healthy. Blockage of this flow causes problems. Ancient Chinese philosophers called this flow Chi. Scientists have verified that complex feedback loops regulate the flow of materials in and out of our cells. This flow, known in biology as homeostasis, moves oxygen into cells and removes waste, as well as regulates other cellular functions.

To locate energy blockages in the body of a patient, Hawkes first tried watching a pendulum held above the body, which would swing back and forth over a blockage. She soon learned, however, to sense blocked areas in a patient's body with her hands.

Emotions and beliefs, as well as physical damage or disease, create blockages in the energy flow within us. Jocelyn, who had been diagnosed with breast cancer and was facing chemotherapy asked Hawkes to help her heal. Hawkes had Jocelyn focus her mind on walking along her favorite beach—listening to the waves, smelling the salt air, and feeling the sun's warmth on her body.

Hawkes saw and helped Joselyn see that her energy blockage was a belief that her cancer was a punishment for doing something wrong. After she used meditation to overcome her anxiety, her emotional blockage ended and a healthier flow of energy helped to heal her body.

Hawkes also helped Elli, who had a cast on her broken leg, by identifying with her hands the energy blockage beneath the cast. She told Elli that the two

92 Joyce Whiteley Hawkes, "Cell-Level Healing: Where Science and Spirit Meet," https://celllevelhealing.com/.

pieces of her broken leg were set improperly. After an X-ray confirmed the error, Elli's doctor properly aligned the bones and put on a new cast. Hawkes then helped Elli focus on her internal energy flow and her leg healed rapidly.

Jeremy had broken his ankle playing soccer, and after removing the cast his doctor had asserted that the ankle had healed. Yet eight months later, Jeremy was limping due to the pain he felt while walking. His doctor explained that bone spurs were causing the pain but offered no remedy. When Hawkes examined his ankle, passing her hands over the injured area, she observed his lower leg beginning to sweat and turn white. She felt "spikes of heat" in her hands, which subsided as she passed her hands over his ankle.

Hawkes explained to Jeremy that osteoclasts were cells in the body that can remodel our bones. These cells may create bone spurs when healing a broken bone but can also remove bone spurs. By passing her hands over his ankle, Hawkes provided energy to his osteoclasts that helped them heal his bone spurs. She taught Jeremy how mentally "to call his osteoclasts into action." By focusing on his osteoclasts, Jeremy helped heal his ankle and was able to play soccer once again.

Hawkes writes that cellular energy flow affects "spiritual, emotional, and physical issues" as well as a person's physical health. She writes: "When Flow reaches all of the levels from Soul to Cell, liveliness enhances simple daily routines. The body responds with improved health."[93]

Hawkes learned from her indigenous teacher in Bali how to help someone accept death. After years of training and practice, she says the feeling in the room changes when a patient is in a coma and their soul leaves the body. The heart and respiration stop within thirty minutes after the soul leaves. A person's consciousness, however, may remain around the body for some time.

Hawkes suggests to those facing the transition from the physical to the spiritual realm that: "The fear of death reduces the fullness of life and holds part of us captive. When we face and overcome our fear of death, we can live in a new dimension of ease, clarity, and vitality."

In Bali, a person training to be a healer may be required to spend the night on a rocky outcrop of land accessible only during low tide. In the dark, as the waves crash on the rocks, cobras come out to investigate the visitor. If she remains silent and calm, the cobras will ignore her.

These practices suggest why indigenous healers are respected in their communities. They are able to cross the gap between the material and spirit worlds to obtain healing information for a dying person or a family. There

93 Joyce Whiteley Hawkes, *Cell-Level Healing*, 35-38.

might be an herb or a ritual that could calm a troubled person. Perhaps, a healing intervention that actually enters the cells of the body and brings remarkable physical healing.

Hawkes says that her ten years of study with Jero Mangku Sri Kandi, her Balinese teacher and mentor, taught her to embrace a greater reality that extends beyond the material world. Her test of courage and meditative stillness involved sitting for twenty minutes beside a busy red ant hill at a remote temple. She did not suffer a single bite. Hawkes says that working with Jero enabled her to help guide individuals into death without relying on Balinese temples or chanting.

Carl was dying from cancer and struggling with unbearable pain. His wife asked Hawkes to help him let go. Hawkes synchronized her breathing and awareness with his. She "journeyed with him into the altered states of consciousness" she had learned to navigate safely. She saw the frightening images confronting him and understood why despite his pain his soul remained in his body.

Hawkes encouraged him to continue toward the light beyond all the illusions. "The energy from this extraordinary light," Hawkes told Carl, is "Divine Love." They went on together until he was free from his decaying body and "soared toward the light."

In July 2005, Hawkes was filmed for a documentary in Dr. Akio Mori's laboratory at Niho University in Tokyo, Japan. The video aired on Nokia TV, Channel 4, in Japan on August 8, 2005. Dr. Mori is a research scientist in the field of brain mapping. After reviewing her 128-sensor EEG data, which was gathered while she sent healing energy to a cancer patient, Dr. Mori noted her extraordinary level of concentration and unusual activity in the left prefrontal cortex—which he identified as the site of happiness.

In June 2006, Dr. Acosta-Urquidi, Ph.D., recorded her brain activity with a portable EEG device while she was in meditation and working with two clients who were sitting about six feet from her. The data showed high levels of "focused delta waves, peaks of beta, and increased alpha during healing," as wellas "high-frequency gamma brainwaves along with high levels of coordinated brain activity."[94]

---

94 Ibid., 150-151. The EEG equipment that Dr. Acosta-Urquidi used was conventional: A Mitsar Instrument (St. Petersburg, Russia) employing a 19-channel electrocap hookup, 10-20 International system, and referential linked ears montage. Raw data was analyzed to yield power-frequency spectra and topographic brain maps (QEEG). .

Hawkes concludes her book, *Cell-Level Healing*, with these encouraging words: "May your own practice of gratitude, clearing, focus, and Cell-Level Healing create your own bridge to connect Soul to Cell and back again, thereby extinguishing any fear of death."[95]

95 Ibid., 142-148.

Visions

British scholar Frederick W. H. Myers (1843-1901), poet and founder of the Society for Psychical Research, documented hundreds of cases in *Human Personality and Its Survival of Bodily Death*, which was published in 1903. In the 1961 edition of the book's introduction, psychologist Jeffrey Mishlove writes: "Myers maintains the human personality is composed of two active coherent streams of thoughts and feelings. Those lying above the ordinary threshold of consciousness he labels supraliminal, while those that remain submerged beneath consciousness are subliminal." Myers described the transition between these two streams of consciousness as our liminal experience. From his research, Myers concluded that: "In many cases the deeper layers seem autonomous and independent of the conscious self."[96]

Some of the cases included in *Human Personality and Its Survival of Bodily Death* would today be described as r*emote viewing*. For instance, M. Badaire, a school director in France, reported this inexplicable vision by a teacher, Theophile Janicaud, who had frequent attacks of somnambulism while living with Badaire.

> Badaire: 'Every evening he got up, walked about the dormitory, descended to the study to work in the dark, or wandered about the gardens for hours at a time, after which he went back to bed. One evening about 11 o'clock Janicaud came knocking at the door of my bedroom.'
>
> Janicaud: 'I have just arrived from Vendome and have come to give you the news of your family. Monsieur and Madame Arnault are well, and your little son has four teeth.'
>
> Badaire: 'Could you go back again and tell me where they are at present?'
>
> Janicaud: 'Wait . . . I am there . . . They are sleeping in a room on the first floor; their bed is at the farther end of the room, to the left. The nurse's bed is to the right, and Henry's cradle close to it.'

96 F. W. H. Myers, *Human Personality and Its Survival of Bodily Death* (Longmans, Green and Co., 1903, 1954; Hampton Roads, 2001).

Badaire: 'The description of the room and the position of the beds were perfectly exact, and the following day I received a letter from my father-in-law telling me that my child had cut his fourth tooth.'

Myers described the history of communicating with the dead by crystal-gazing (*scrying*) which was practiced throughout the ancient world—in Egypt, Assyria, Persia, Greece, Rome, India, China, Japan, by Native North Americans, the Incas, by Africans of the Fez and Zulu cultures, by Polynesians, shamans in Eastern Russia and Siberia, and in Madagascar.[97] He also noted an event verifying the extraordinary visionary ability of Emanuel Swedenborg (1688-1772), which German philosopher Immanuel Kant (1724-1804) reported in his 1766 book, *Dreams of a Spirit Seer*:

"The widow of the Dutch Ambassador at Stockholm was called upon by a goldsmith to pay for a silver service that her husband had purchased before his death. She believed it had been paid for but could not find the receipt; she begged Swedenborg to ask her husband where it was. Three days later he came to her house and informed her in the presence of some visitors that he had conversed with her husband and had learnt from him that the debt had been paid, and the receipt was in a bureau in an upstairs room. The spirit had said that after pulling out the left-hand drawer a board would appear, and on drawing this out a secret compartment would be disclosed, containing his private Dutch correspondence and the receipt. The whole company went up the stairs and the papers were found, as described, in the secret compartment, of which no one had known before."[98]

Henry James, Sr., father of the novelist Henry James and the philosopher and psychologist William James, accepted Swedenborg's teachings about Christian faith and the afterlife and raised his sons on the basis of Swedenborg's visions. As an adult, William James (1842-1910), joined Myers in leading the Society for Psychic Research, despite scholarly opposition in the United States to his participation in the organization.

James describes experimenting with his own conscious experience. "Some years ago, I myself made observations [regarding] nitrous oxide intoxication and reported them in print. One conclusion was forced upon my mind at that time, and my impression of its truth has ever since remained unshaken. It is that our normal waking consciousness, rational consciousness as we call it, is but one special type of consciousness, whilst all about it, parted from it by the flimsiest of screens, there lie potential forms of consciousness entirely differ-

97 Ibid., 78, 88-89, 169, 130.
98 Ibid, 299.

ent. We may go through life without suspecting their existence; but apply the requisite stimulus, and at a touch they are there in all their completeness, definite types of mentality that probably somewhere have their field of application and adaptation. No account of the universe in its totality can be final which leaves these other forms of consciousness quite disregarded."[99]

Polish engineer Stefan Ossowiecki (1877-1944) as a child growing up in Moscow where his father had a chemical business, saw *bands of color* around people, now known as *auras*. After the Bolshevik Revolution his family's property was confiscated; he was imprisoned and threatened with death. In a 1937 interview he stated that "the experience of arrest, enforced isolation, and the threat of death was a watershed in his spiritual development," and the development of his psychic powers. "It was only then," he recalls, "that I appreciated this gift, given to me by the Creator, and understood that I can help others using it."[100]

His gift was tested many times. Ossowiecki claimed 'time and space did not exist in the superconscious state' that allowed him to view past events. In a 2017 book, *The Secrets Vaults of Time: Psychic Archaeology and the Quest for Man's Beginnings*, researcher Stephan A. Schwartz reports that Ossowiecki: "told his friends that while he did not go into a trance, when he moved into his superconscious mind, this became his primary level of awareness." After this transition, "it was as if he were looking at a movie running in reverse; that is, from most recent to more distant events of the past.

"When he chose, he could freeze this reverse action. As that happened, it was as if he were suddenly in an airplane, first seeing a sort of broad overview, and then going lower until he was approximately at a point of view where his eye would normally be if he were physically standing on the spot he had chosen in the past. At this stage the action would begin again, only now going forward as it should."[101]

Mayer's 2008 book, *Extraordinary Knowing*, includes examples of inexplicable visions including the remote viewing ability of Joe McMoneagle. Stanford Research Institute (SRI) scientist Harold Puthoff, hired to coordinate a federal government remote-viewing project, told Mayer that McMoneagle

99 Leonard Gibson, "Amplified Subject," in John H. Buchannan, author, and Christopher M. Aanstoos, editor, *Rethinking Consciousness: Extraordinary Challenges for Contemporary Science* (Process Century Press, 2020).

100 Stefan Ossowiecki, "All About Heaven," https://allaboutheaven.org/sources/ossowiecki-stefan/190.

101 Stephan A. Schwartz, *The Secret Vaults of Time: Psychic Archaeology and the Quest for Man's Beginnings* (Open Road Distribution, 2017), 229-230.

was invited to participate. Puthoff recalls that when McMoneagle was given only the geographic coordinates of a location, he saw large buildings in a frozen environment near the sea.

Here is McMoneagle's account of his remote viewing. "I spent some time relaxing and emptying my mind. Then with my eyes closed, I imagined myself drifting down into the building, passing downward through its roof. The building was easily the size of two or three huge shopping centers, all under a single roof. In giant bays were what looked like cigars of different sizes, sitting in gigantic racks. Thick mazes of scaffolding and interlocking steel pipes were everywhere. Within these were what appeared to be two large cylinders being welded side to side, and I had an overwhelming sense that this was a really big submarine, with twin hulls."

After a second remote viewing visit inside the facility, McMoneagle created a detailed drawing of what he'd seen. His report for the National Security Council proved to be incredibly accurate.[102] McMoneagle attributes his remote viewing ability to an earlier near-death experience.[103]

Physicist Russell Targ, a cofounder with Puthoff of SRI, reports in his 2010 book, *Limitless Mind: A Guide to Remote Viewing and Transformation of Consciousness*: "We now know that our timeless awareness has mobility independent of our physical body. The evidence is very strong that awareness, which is what we are, can receive an inflow of information from all of space-time, and can generate an outflow of healing intention to the present, the future, and the past. This all happens because space-time is nonlocal and there is no separation in consciousness."[104]

Psychiatrist Raymond Moody, in his 2010 book, *Glimpses of Eternity: Sharing a Loved One's Passage from This Life to the Next*, relates the following experience of Lin Jacquin when she was seven years old.

Jacquin was lying in the hospital with bandaged eyes, recovering from eye surgery, when she "saw" a light and a boy walking out of it. It was Jimmy, a school classmate. He told Lin that he couldn't find his way home and asked her to help him. Jacquin says they walked together into the light until he was back home. She learned later that Jimmy had been struck and killed by a car on the same day she had her eye surgery.[105]

---

102 Elizabeth Lloyd Mayer, *Extraordinary Knowing*, 110-127.

103 Marilyn Schlitz, *Death Makes Life Possible: Revolutionary Insights on Living, Dying, and the Continuation of Consciousness* (Sounds True, 2015), 52-55.

104 Russell Targ, *Limitless Mind: A Guide to Remote Viewing and Transformation of Consciousness* (New World Library, 2010), 101.

105 Raymond Moody, *Glimpses of Eternity*, 63.

Pediatrician Melvin Morse in his 1994 book, *Parting Visions: Pre-Death Visions and Spiritual Experiences*, writes that W. Dewi Rees, a physician in Wales, published research in the *British Medical Journal* describing the visions of widows and widowers in Wales. Rees reported that a majority of those who participated in his study experienced contact with their deceased spouses. Most of the subjects in this study were happy to have "the company of their dead spouse." Rees also verified that those who enjoyed the presence of their deceased spouse were less likely to die in the year after their spouse's death.

Frank Oski, professor of pediatrics at Johns Hopkins University, shared with Morse his own experience as a medical student, when he was frustrated by the deaths of children dying of congenital defects. After falling asleep, Oski was awakened by a bright light shining in his room. He saw the shape of a young woman with wings on her back. She explained to Oski that some of these children had been asked to teach those who care for them how to be more loving. The angel added, "It stretches our own humanity to love a child who is less than perfect, and that is an important lesson for us."[106]

D. Goren Grip, a Swedish anesthesiologist, told Morse that at age five he was hospitalized for a minor surgical procedure. The anesthesiologist inadvertently gave him too much ether, which caused his breathing to stop. As he lay unconscious on the operating table, he saw a being of light on a road in front of him. Grip felt a strong love emanating from the being, as he experienced a review of his short life.

Grip's life was transformed by this experience. The message of unconditional love and giving that he received from the being of light led him to become a doctor. Despite the positive aspects of his near-death experience, Grip knew the professional difficulties of discussing his vision with colleagues. As he wryly observed, "I have had the typical problems of someone who is transformed but is living in a world which is not."

Morse reports the case of Martha, mother of four children, who lost two of them in a car accident. In the funeral home, preparing their bodies for burial, she noticed her own mother (who had died a year earlier) standing next to her. Her mother was smiling as she gently touched her granddaughter's body. "They are with me now," she said to Martha. "I'll take care of them."[107]

In his 2012 book, *Paranormal: My Life in Pursuit of the Afterlife*, Moody reports on his *scrying* (apparition) experiments. The first subject was a forty-four-year-old nurse whose husband died from a heart attack two years earlier. Before she entered the apparition booth, Moody spent several hours talking

106 Melvin Morse, *Parting Visions*, 15-16, 21-22.
107 Ibid., 102-105, 119.

with her about her husband. Yet, when she came out of the apparition booth, she said she had seen her deceased father instead. He had even stepped out of the mirror to speak with her.

A woman hoping to see her grandmother was amazed not only to see her but also to be embraced by her. Moody reports after several hundred apparition experiences, more than 80% of those who entered the apparition environment said they "saw departed loved ones."[108]

Moody ended his book, *Reunions*, with the following report. A woman hoping to see her son, who had died of cancer two years earlier, saw memories from his childhood and sensed his presence. A few days later, however, she woke up in the night and found her son standing in her bedroom. She stood up and they talked together for some time. Before leaving, he gave her a hug and even lifted her off the ground. She told Moody, "I now feel as though I can put my son's death behind me and get on fully with my life."[109]

Moody concludes, "Whether these techniques just access a place in our consciousness where memories of our deceased relative exist or actually extend our reach into the supernatural world is not the issue. On a human level *scrying* is a successful treatment of the paralyzing psychological problem of grief."[110]

Steve Jobs, inventor and co-founder of Apple, was diagnosed with cancer in 2003 and died eight years later at the age of 56. His sister, Mona Simpson, a novelist and professor of English, who spoke at his memorial service, ended her eulogy by sharing his last words. "Oh Wow. Oh Wow. Oh Wow."[111]

Ptolemy Tompkins, in his 2012 book *The Modern Book of the Dead*, writes that the nineteenth century psychical researcher, Frederick Myers, proposed the word *imaginal* to describe a state of mind that could be understood as both real and imaginary. Tompkins suggests we might conceive of this state of consciousness as, "A plane of experience that is every bit as real as the physical world we experience in our physical bodies but that is also much more elastic; a world that blooms and buzzes a hundredfold more vividly and intensely—and personally—than the one we are in right now."

If we link this imaginal dimension with evidence that the mind is not simply a product of the brain, we have: "A perspective on the fate not just of con-

108 Raymond Moody, *Paranormal*, 197-198, 226.

109 Raymond Moody, *Reunions*, 206-208.

110 Raymond Moody, *Paranormal*, 226-227.

111 Mona Simpson, "A Sister's Eulogy for Steve Jobs," *The New York Times*, Oct. 30, 2011, https://www.nytimes.com/2011/10/30/opinion/mona-simpsons-eulogy-for-steve-jobs.html.

sciousness, but of our particular, individual, personal consciousness after the body has been left behind. A perspective that allows us to continue to believe in the existence of the spirit in the age of science, and that allows us also to appreciate different spiritual perspectives without insisting that one be right and all the others wrong."[112]

112 Ptolemy Tompkins, *The Modern Book of the Dead* (Atria Books, 2012), 112-113.

Dreams

Human Personality and Its Survival of Bodily Death published in 1903 by the Society for Psychical Research includes many cases of dreams that Frederick Myers identified as reflecting subliminal consciousness. Rev. P. H. Newnham, who described himself as *an utter skeptic*, reported this surprising dream to Myers:

"In March 1854, I was up in Oxford, keeping my last term, in lodgings. I was subject to violent neuralgic headaches, which always culminated in sleep. One evening, about 8 pm, I had an unusually violent one; when it became unendurable, I went into my bedroom and flung myself, without undressing, on the bed, and soon fell asleep.

"I then had a singularly clear and vivid dream, all the incidents of which are still as clear to my memory as ever. I dreamed that I was visiting with the family of the lady who subsequently became my wife. As I bid members of the family good night, I perceived that my fiancée was near the top of the staircase. I rushed upstairs, overtook her on the top step, and passed my two arms round her waist, under her arms, from behind.

"On this I woke, and a clock in the house struck ten almost immediately afterwards. So strong was the impression of the dream that I wrote a detailed account of it the next morning to my fiancée. Crossing my letter, not in answer to it, I received a letter from the lady in question: 'Were you thinking about me, very specially, last night, just about ten? For, as I was going upstairs to bed, I distinctly heard your footsteps on the stairs, and felt you put your arms round my waist.'"[113]

Samuel Clemens (who published as Mark Twain) joined the American Society for Psychical Research when he was seeking an explanation for an extraordinary dream. Leonard Gibson relates Clemens' experience in an essay entitled "Amplified Subject," published in the 2020 book, *Rethinking Consciousness: Extraordinary Challenges for Contemporary Science*.

In 1858 the Clemens brothers, Sam and Henry, were working on the Mississippi River and training on a steam-powered paddle-wheeler called the Pennsylvania. One evening when the boat was in Saint Louis, the brothers went ashore to see their sister. Henry returned to the boat, but Sam spent the

113 F. W. H. Myers, *Human Personality and Its Survival of Bodily Death*, 78.

night at his sister's. While asleep, he dreamed of seeing Henry's body lying in a casket, resting on two chairs. White roses, and a single red one, were on Henry's chest.

In the morning upon returning to the boat Sam confirmed that his brother was fine, but the captain had assigned Sam to another boat that was to follow the Pennsylvania. Three days later, when nearing Memphis, the Pennsylvania's boiler exploded. More than a hundred people were injured or killed. As soon as Sam learned of the explosion, he rode a rented horse to Memphis.

That night Henry died of his injuries. The next morning, Sam walked into a room where Henry's body lay in a casket resting on two chairs. As Sam watched, a woman walked to the coffin and placed upon his brother's chest a bouquet of white roses with a single red rose.[114]

Deborah Blum in her 2007 book, *Ghost Hunters: William James and the Search for Scientific Proof of Life After Death*, reports that William James published an account of a missing girl whose body was only found because a woman named Nellie Titus, living five miles away, "dreamed of where the child was trapped underwater beside a bridge. Her description enabled a diver to find the body, despite his lengthy but unsuccessful attempts days before." James concluded that the Titus case "is a decidedly solid document in favor of the admission of a supernormal faculty of seership."[115]

Morse records stories of children who dreamed about dying before they died. Toby was three years old when he entered the hospital where Rosemarie worked. He was in remission from leukemia and one day told Rosemarie about a recent dream of going on a trip. She encouraged him to draw it, and with crayons he drew a picture that was dark gray and blue on the left side. On the right side he included white and yellow flowers, a blue bird, and a few other pet animals.

"Soon I'm going to a special place," he told Rosemary. To get there he would have to go through a dark tunnel, but he wasn't scared because he knew how beautiful it was on the other side. When Rosemary asked him when he was going, he said "pretty soon." Within a week, Toby died.

Another boy who was dying of cancer told his nurse that he'd asked God if he could live another year. He'd explained to God that he wanted his three-

114 Leonard Gibson, "Amplified Subject," *Rethinking Consciousness*.

115 Deborah Blum, *Ghost Hunters: William James and the Search for Scientific Proof of Life After Death* (Penguin, 2007).

year-old brother to be old enough to accept his death. Given his condition, the nurse thought he was unlikely to live that long. He did, however, live a year before dying.[116]

In his 2013 book *Glimpses of Eternity*, Moody relates another extraordinary dream. A seventeen-year-old boy named Shane had been hit by a truck and died in the hospital. When his parents arrived back home from the hospital, their deaf fifteen-year-old daughter told them she'd dreamed of traveling with Shane to visit heaven. Shane told his sister that their aunt was pregnant with a boy, a fact unknown to their parents.[117] When this information was later confirmed, the subjective experience of the dream became objectively verified evidence of an afterlife experience.

Dr. Allan Hamilton, early in his medical career, served as a surgical fellow in the African country of Gabon at the hospital founded by Albert Schweitzer on the Ogooué River. This experience included in his 2009 book, *The Scalpel and the Soul: Encounters with Surgery, the Supernatural, and the Healing Power of Hope*, taught him to be open to the supernatural.

Hamilton was asked to travel down the river with a member of the Fang tribe named Jean-Michael, to bring vaccines to villages along the way. The day they were to depart, their small dugout canoe was not where they expected it to be. They eventually found it, but with the motor missing. Locating another motor took a long time, delaying their departure to the next day.

After several hours on the river, they came to a fork and had to make a choice. Hamilton was shocked when he learned that Jean-Michael didn't know which fork to take.

Hamilton remembers feeling overwhelmed with anxiety. They had no map to follow and no radio by which to ask for instructions. He imagined that this was how people became lost in the wilds of Africa. Unsure of what to do, they steered the canoe to the shore, climbed up the bank, and collapsed onto a tangle of vines and roots.

Suddenly, a small man appeared from behind a tree, wearing only shorts and a necklace of coins. His muscles stood out like ropes on his lean body. His hair was grayish-white and curly, and a leather sack hung from his shoulder with something inside that was wiggling.

Jean-Michael made introductions and explained that they were bringing medicine to the village of Tan-Beang. The stranger then shared, in broken

116 Melvin Morse, *Parting Visions*, 65-67, 100, 108.

117 Raymond Moody, *Glimpses of Eternity*, 67-68.

French, that he had dreamed they would come the day before to Tan-Beang, his village. In the dream, however, the two men became lost and did not know the way, and he was asked to await them beside the river, and then guide them.

"Who asked you to stand here?" Hamilton said.

The stranger repeated that in his dream he was to meet the men yesterday, and when they didn't come, he waited. Hamilton realized that "invisible forces" and not the flowing water of the river had brought them to this stranger who would guide them to his village on the river.

French Catholic missionaries who roamed Gabon when it was a colony had named this man David, but his real name was Quteen which in his native language of Fang means "who sees things." Which he certainly did. Hamilton suggests that finding the village, or more accurately being found and led to the village, should not be understood as a coincidence. It was not the result of random events. Instead, it should be recognized as intentional.

Wasn't Outeen's appearance meant to occur? Wasn't the best explanation that he "had been willed" to be there? If so, then their safe arrival should be recognized as a gift. The lesson for Hamilton was not that they were found. The more striking meaning was that their purpose to deliver medicine to the village was "interwoven with a complete stranger's dream," which enabled them to fulfill their purpose.

Henry David Thoreau, Hamilton says, wrote it was never too late to reject prejudice. On the Ogooué River in Gabon, Hamilton accepted this gift. "Outeen's conviction that he must wait to lead us to the village had been true. Now events were unfolding as they were supposed to. It was simply undeniable to me that I was 'in debt' to his dream. I felt gratitude that something, some force, had sent him to help us." Of course, Hamilton observed, it is easier to accept the claim of supernatural forces when in a culture where this belief is common sense.

In Africa, Hamilton lost his uncritical belief in science, and instead began to appreciate the power of dreams, magic, taboos, and curses. "Africa taught me that the supernatural lies just beneath the surface." Openness to experience would likely verify what Africans understood to be self-evident.

"In the final analysis, superstitions, omens, and intuitions are the reflections of a conscious effort on the part of an individual to detect the subtle signals sent to us from the natural world. If we are open to subtlety, then the world resonates with significance."[118]

---

118 Allan Hamilton, *The Scalpel and the Soul*, 13-28.

Mystical Experiences

I begin this section with Bob Berman's story because he was both a science student and not religious at the time of his experience. Those who write about mystical experiences often focus on religious or spiritual communities or ascetic practices. Yet, what have been called mystical experiences can happen to anyone, as Berman attests, and they are more common than we imagine. These overwhelming moments often involve experiencing unity with all that is, with some persons receiving a huge download of information that they know is coming from outside of their lives. Experiences identified as mystical also may involve an astonishing sense of being loved or liberated.

Bob Berman, co-author with Robert Lanza of their 2008 book, *Beyond Biocentrism: Rethinking Time, Space, Consciousness, and the Illusion of Death,* explains that as a junior in college he was studying for a test in his physiology course when something he read in his text concerning the visual part of the brain triggered "a split-second insight that the distinction between *external* and *internal* is unreal."

"An enormous weight I'd never realized I had borne was suddenly lifted. An experience began that no words could convey. It was ineffable and life-altering. The best I can say is that 'I' was suddenly gone, replaced by the certainty of being the entire cosmos. There was absolute peace. I knew with total confidence, not logically—because, as I said, Bob was no longer present—that birth and death do not exist. That all is perfect eternally, that time is unreal, and that all is one. The joy was beyond anything I could have imagined. The to-the-marrow certainty could perhaps be better described as a recognition, an ancient familiarity of being Home."

When his intense initial experience faded, he was back in his room with his textbooks. Except, he was no longer an observer of the world. "It was as if my consciousness had previously been long confined, like a canary in a little cage, and that a false sense of being a separate, isolated, thinking individual had now vanished.

"When a person came into view, I was this person. The universe was one entity for all time. There were not billions of humans and animals. There was one living, deathless entity. (And no, in case you're wondering, this experience was not chemically induced.)

"This experience lasted three weeks, during which time no thought flitted across my consciousness. But eventually the ongoing stream of mental chatter, of being an individual, an observer, returned—accompanied by loss of the peace and oneness. It felt terrible."

Afterward, he went overseas, traveling mostly in the East. He read spiritual books and tried everything. He had spiritual moments but never again had the full experience. He did learn that nearly everyone has had moments of being "out of oneself" and "becoming the object observed." On January 26, 1976, *The New York Times* magazine published an article including results of a survey verifying that a quarter of those surveyed have experienced "a sense of the unity of everything."[119]

Sociologist Mike Sosteric unexpectedly experienced an immense and overwhelming download of information about religion and spirituality. This shocked him, as just two days earlier he had raged at God for allowing so much suffering in the world—as if God really did exist. Much earlier in life Sosteric had rejected his childhood Catholic Church experience and was intellectually a Marxist and an atheist when he *received* surprising and convincing information that verified reality's spiritual dimension.

"Suddenly, I was having multiple noetic experiences and writing, as a consequence of these noetic experiences, poems, parables, books, and stories about things I had never even thought about before. The very first thing that came spewing from my brain was a story of creation in the form of an epic poem! This story of creation replaced the canonical creation mythology of good and evil with a story of true unity and purpose.

"A decade and a half later," he writes, "I still sit down every day and let it flow. When I first started, I would put in about an hour a day. Now it is closer to four or five hours a day, with a much more rigorous approach, and a much more diverse output of scholarly articles, poems, books, and educational materials."

The information pouring into Sosteric's mind included a description of the features of mystical experiences, which fit his experience. The word *noetic* refers to a powerful feeling that the information being received is absolutely true. Sosteric adds that with the information he suddenly received, there was also a shift in interest and a change in expertise. His entire belief system was transformed in just a few days. He began reading about mystics, such as the theosophical author Madame Blavatsky who also *received* much of what she wrote without having to learn it.

---

119 Robert Lanza and Bob Berman, *Beyond Biocentrism: Rethinking Time Space, Consciousness, and the Illusion of Death* (BenBella Books, 2016), 110-111.

Sosteric knew that he was connecting to something that he called the *fabric of consciousness*. His "powerful mystical experiences" gave him so much information that fifteen years later he is still working through it. Sosteric realized that his noetic experience had destroyed the materialist worldview that as a scientist he had taken for granted. Instead, he now experienced "consciousness as a cosmic Internet."[120]

As a sociologist, Sosteric considered his experience as a new way to conceptualize Abraham Maslow's *peak experiences*. Unlike Maslow, however, who used scientific concepts—perhaps to avoid controversy from academic colleagues—Sosteric directly addresses the issue of *authentic spirituality*, arguing that it helps us connect to a Fabric of Consciousness that exists independently of physical existence.[121]

Sosteric clarifies his own spiritual experience by endorsing Einstein's support for "a relationship to the cosmos, God, and creation fueled not by fear or existential angst, but by authentic, spiritual experience."[122]

For years, Laura Lynne Jackson led two separate lives. In one she was a graduate of Oxford University teaching English in high school. In another she was a medium helping those grieving over the death of loved ones to communicate with them. Then one day at the school where she taught, she experienced an immense download of information "from the universe."

To verify her extraordinary ability, Jackson submitted to rigorous tests with the nonprofit Forever Family Foundation, a science-based group that helps people in grief, and then with the Windbridge Institute for Applied Research in Human Potential. At Windbridge, Jackson says, she completed an eight-step, quintuple-blind screening test administered by scientists to become one of only a small group of Certified Research Mediums.

"I am clairvoyant," she explains, "which means I have the ability to gather information about people and events through means other than my five senses. I'm also clairaudient—I can perceive sounds through means other than my ears—and clairsentient, which allows me to feel things through nonhuman means."

---

120 Mike Sosteric, "Mysticism, Consciousness, Death," *Journal of Consciousness Exploration & Research*, Dec. 2016, vol. 7, issue 11, 1099-1118.

121 Mike Sosteric, *Rocket Scientists' Guide to Authentic Spirituality* (Lightning Path Press, 2010), 9.

122 Mike Sosteric, "Three Interesting Things Einstein Said About God and Religion," *The Lightning Strike*, Sep. 12, 2019, https://medium.com/human-spirituality/three-interesting-things-einstein-said-about-god-and-religion-11798a4e23d7, 3.

Jeff Tarrant, a researcher at the University of Missouri, performed an EEG study of Jackson while she was engaged in contacting a deceased child on the Other Side. He reported that her EEG had a pattern of brain waves usually identified as reflecting a coma or deep sleep. "This made sense to me," Jackson writes. "When I do a reading, my ego dissolves, and I connect with something greater than myself."

Jackson says that the "Other Side" has shown her "that we comprise a massive field of light—it cannot exist without us. But neither can we individually exist outside this field. Our existence is primarily defined by our place in this grand constellation of energy, not by who we are individually. We may appear to exist separately from anyone else, and we may perceive the boundaries that describe us and feel we are autonomous. But our energy, our consciousness, is inexorably entangled with the energy of others.

"To me, that is better evidence of our interconnected existence than any scientific experiment could ever provide. We are all invested in each other's fates and fortunes. To the world, you may be one person. But to one person, you may be the world."[123]

Fenwicks' book, *The Truth in the Light*, reports that over a third of people, based on an enormous sample of 45 million, have said that they have "had a mystical experience." By definition, a mystical experience originates "in a transcendental reality." Doing a simple calculation, the Fenwicks suggest that in this survey almost sixteen million people reported experiencing what many near-death survivors call a spiritual reality.[124]

In Eastern cultures, where Hindu and Buddhist images and practices arose and were nurtured, the word *mystical* is rarely used to describe what in Western cultures is described as a life-transforming experience. Instead we find references to awakening, or being enlightened, or pure awareness, or realizing suddenly that the ordinary world is also an extraordinary world.

Deepak Chopra, who was born in India but trained as a physician in the West, now practices and teaches meditation based on Hindu insights. "I grew up to put on a Western-style suit and step around saints on the sidewalk," he admits, "but as I looked deeper into the issues of mind-body medicine, I kept returning to India's ancient traditions."

Chopra asserts that the ancient Hindu saints, known as *rishis*, "were just as capable as we are of dividing up nature into space, time, matter, and energy." Instead of relying on these scientific concepts, however, they realized that the

---

123 Laura Lynne Jackson, *The Light Between Us: Stories from Heaven* (Spiegal & Grau, 2015).

124 Peter and Elizabeth Fenwick, *The Truth in the Light*, 22-24.

gap between conscious awareness and sleep offered a possible experience of the "underlying layer of unity in nature." The *rishis* found that this space in between two ordinary states of consciousness could be experienced through the practice of yoga meditation, when the mind transcends its ordinary consciousness and is therefore open to inclusive, extraordinary experience.

"The brain is not important as an object," the *rishis* argue. The brain is only important "because our own subjectivity shines through it; when our brains show us the world, they are really showing us ourselves.

"Many things *out there* don't exist for us, not because they are unreal, but because *in here* we have not shaped the brain to perceive them. We are like radios that appear to have all the channels when actually they are stuck on three—waking, sleep, and dreaming." The *rishis* learned that "only when the mind stops thinking [is it able to] return to its source in silence and then to touch pure awareness."[125]

In Chopra's 2023 book entitled *Living in the Light*, co-authored with Sarah-Platt Finger, Director of Yoga at the Chopra Foundation, we find this comparison of Western spiritual thinking and the Hindu yoga that Chopra recommends for transforming your life.

"Take a moment to visualize some specific ways that might make your day more satisfying. Perhaps a friend tells you a piece of good news, you complete a project at work, or you watch your child or spouse smile at you and you feel a rush of love.

"If you rewind these experiences and evaluate them through the prism of Yoga, each event might look the same on the surface. But if you practice Royal Yoga (Chopra's term for Hindu *Raja Yoga*), what happens inside is transformed: *You find that you are living in the light.* The effect is all-embracing, because if there is life, there should be light.

Chopra says that the word light carries a religious implication for many. "A Christian might think of the phrase, D*on't hide your light under a bushel basket* or Jesus saying to his disciples, *You are the light of the world.*"

In Royal Yoga, however, "Light is pure awareness; it is the cosmic consciousness that creates and maintains the universe and everything in it. In practical terms, living in the light is about living consciously, and the ultimate goal in life is to live only in the light, having cast off every form of ignorance, pain, and suffering."[126]

---

125 Deepak Chopra, *Quantum Healing: Exploring the Frontiers of Mind/Body Healing* (Bantam, 2015), 206, 212-213.

126 Deepak Chopra and Sarah Platt-Finger, *Living in the Light* (Harmony/Rodale, Kindle Edition, 2023), 4-5.

Chopra uses contemporary science to explain how he has adapted an ancient Hindu meditation practice for English-speaking individuals who are drawn to practicing yoga. For instance, in his 2017 book co-authored with physicist Menas Kafatos, *You Are the Universe: Discovering Your Cosmic Self and Why It Matters*, the authors explain why *light* is inexplicable and why this affects how we see reality. [127]

The Dalai Lama dialogues with scientists to interpret to contemporary Westerners the Tibetan Buddhist practice. In his 2005 book *The Universe in a Single Atom*, he explains, "Two features—luminosity, or clarity, and knowing, or cognizance—have come to characterize *the mental* in Indo-Tibetan Buddhist thought. *Clarity* here refers to the ability of mental states to reveal or reflect. *Knowing*, by contrast, refers to mental states' faculty to perceive or apprehend what appears."

He acknowledges that conceptualizing these features is not easy but suggests this is because: "We are dealing with phenomena that are subjective and internal rather than material objects that may be measured in spatiotemporal terms. Perhaps it is because of these difficulties—the limits of language in dealing with the subjective—that many of the early Buddhist texts explain the nature of consciousness in terms of metaphors such as light or a flowing river. As the primary feature of light is to illuminate, so consciousness is said to illuminate its objects. Just as in light there is no categorical distinction between the illumination and that which illuminates, so in consciousness there is no real difference between the process of knowing or cognition and that which knows or cognizes."

The Dalai Lama explains this significant distinction. "What occurs during meditative contemplation in a tradition such as Buddhism and what occurs during introspection in the ordinary sense are two quite different things. In the context of Buddhism, introspection is employed with careful attention to the dangers of extreme subjectivism—such as fantasies and delusions—and with the cultivation of a disciplined state of mind. Refinement of attention, in terms of stability and vividness, is a crucial preparation for the utilization of rigorous introspection."

Finally, he clarifies that Buddhist meditation is not simply emptying the mind, or a relaxation practice. Nor is its goal a *mysterious or mystical state of ecstasy open only to a few gifted individuals*. Instead, "this process can be compared with rigorous empirical observation." Like careful science.[128]

---

127 Deepak Chopra and Menas C. Kafatos, *You Are the Universe: Discovering Your Cosmic Self and Why It Matters* (Harmony, 2017), 2.

128 Dalai Lama, *The Universe in a Single Atom: The Convergence of Science and Spirituality* (Morgan Road Books, 2005), 124-125, 136, 142.

In China and Japan, Buddhist teaching and practice often emphasized sudden awakening, using koans to stimulate a sudden shift from an ordinary understanding to a more transforming awareness. Physicist Evan Harris Walker (1935-2006), in his 2000 book *The Physics of Consciousness: Quantum Minds and the Meaning of Life*, includes several *koans* that he found helpful in his meditative practice.

To fully grasp the richness of Zen thinking, Walker asserts that we must confront and appreciate something expressed by the eighth-century Zen master Ch'ing-Yuan: "Before you study Zen, mountains are mountains and rivers are rivers. While you study Zen, mountains are no longer mountains and rivers no longer rivers. When you have obtained enlightenment, mountains are again mountains and rivers are again rivers."[129]

Peter Fenwick, who has also experimented with Zen practice, adds: "If you want to follow the Zen path and enter the Zen temple you have to remember that the path is a pathless path and the gate a gateless gate. Or to put it another way, the fact that you maintain or are attached to a goal, the goal of *Kensho*, means that you will never attain it."[130]

---

129 Evan Harris Walker, *The Physics of Consciousness: The Quantum Mind and the Meaning of Life* (Perseus Books 2000), 142.

130 Peter Fenwick, *Shining Light on Transcendence: The Unconventional Journey of a Neuroscientist* (White Crow Books, Kindle Edition, 2019), 35.

Part IV

Scientific Mysteries

In a 2023 book entitled *Why? The Purpose of the Universe*, Philip Goff, a professor of philosophy at Durham University, writes that the scientific community has yet to face that " the challenge posed by consciousness is radically unlike any of the other tasks of science. The reason is that consciousness is not publicly observable."[131]

The Galileo Commission report asserts, "insights from near-death experiences and other transformative experiences suggest that we are all embedded within a larger field of consciousness, with profound implications for ethics in an interconnected world."[132]

The Manifesto for a Post-Materialist Science asserts, "Mind is fundamental in the universe, i.e. it cannot be derived from matter and reduced to anything more basic." Also, "near-death experiences in cardiac arrest suggest that the brain acts as a transceiver of mental activity, i.e. the mind can work through the brain, but is not produced by it. Near-death experiences occurring in cardiac arrest, coupled with evidence from research mediums, further suggest the survival of consciousness, following bodily death, and the existence of other levels of reality that are non-physical."[133]

Subjectivity, purpose and meaning, nature and God also elude scientific explanations, as these human experiences rely on diverse states of consciousness. As we will see, consciousness is fundamental.

131 Phillip Goff, *Why? The Purpose of the Universe* (Oxford University Press, 2023), 77.
132 https://icrl.org/galileo-commission-report/.
133 https://opensciences.org/about/manifesto-for-a-post-materialist-science?

Consciousness and Subjectivity

We are conscious creatures as well as physical bodies. Physics, however, cannot describe or model our consciousness. Physicist Paul Davies, author of the 2008 book, The Goldilocks Enigma: *Why Is the Universe Just Right for Life*, explains: "The laws of physics are simple mathematical relationships expressible with very little information." These laws are universal and apply to all matter and energy, but they are unable to describe living organisms, because even "the genome of the smallest known bacterium contains millions of bits of information" that are "not encoded in the laws of physics." Therefore, "life as we observe it today is 1% physics and 99% history."[134]

Neurosurgeon Wilder Penfield (1891-1976), while performing brain surgery on awake patients who suffered from epileptic fits, used a gentle electric current to find the neural tissue triggering their seizures. Surgically removing this tissue ended the suffering of three quarters of his patients. From these surgeries, Penfield also learned that "even large removals of the cerebral cortex could be carried out without abolishing consciousness," whereas "injury or interference with function in the higher brain-stem, even in small areas, would abolish consciousness completely."

He also discovered that probing neurons in the cerebral cortex triggered flashbacks in his patients, as "when a mother told me she was suddenly aware, as my electrode touched the cortex, of being in her kitchen listening to the voice of her little boy who was playing outside in the yard. She was aware of the neighborhood noises, such as passing motor cars, that might mean danger to him." Penfield found, however, that "successive stimulations of the same point" in the cerebral cortex led to different sorts of "flashbacks."[135] In other words, he verified that memories were not stored in particular locations of the brain. Instead, memories were dispersed and yet could be recalled.

After years of "striving to explain the mind on the basis of brain-action alone," Penfield came to accept that "mechanisms within the human brain" could not account for the "action of the mind." He wrote, "Mind comes into action and goes out of action with the highest brain-mechanism" and also has

134 Paul Davies, *The Goldilocks Enigma: Why is the Universe Just Right for Life?* (Mariner Books, 2008), 233.

135 Wilder Penfield, *The Mystery of the Mind: A Critical Study of Consciousness and the Human Brain* (Princeton University Press, 1975), 19-22

a "form of that energy" differing from the *neuronal potentials* that cause reflex actions in the body. We experience our mind in many different ways but never as brain neurons firing. [136]

A year before his death, in his 1975 book, *The Mystery of the Mind: A Critical Study of Consciousness and the Human Brain*, Penfield affirmed, "The mind is aware of what is going on. The mind reasons and makes new decisions. It understands. It acts as though endowed with an energy of its own. It can make decisions and put them into effect by calling upon various brain mechanisms."

Yet, he did not find any place "in the cerebral cortex where electrical stimulation will cause a patient to believe or to decide." Pause to ponder this striking statement. Believing and deciding are crucial aspects of our conscious experience, but Penfield could not verify a location for these experiences in the brains he studied. This led him to affirm our everyday experience that, "our being does consist of two fundamental elements," one mental and the other physical.[137]

Neurophysiologist Benjamin Libet (1916-2007) relied on the research of Penfield, agreeing "that a person's report of a conscious experience should be regarded as primary evidence." The National Institutes of Health, however, denied his initial grant request, asserting that his proposal to study subjective experience "was not studying a suitable subject."[138]

Physicist Marcelo Gleiser writes in 2021: "Benjamin Libet's pioneering experiments in the 1980s using EEG and more recent ones using fMRI or implants directly into neurons found that the motor region responsible for making a motion, in response to a question, fired up before the subject was aware of it."

Some scientists concluded that Libet had verified that there is no such thing as free will. Gleiser explains, however, that more recent research "has shown the brain activity most highly correlated with decision-making happens simultaneously with the awareness of the choice. There is no neuroscientific reason," Gleiser asserts, "to doubt the reality of free will."[139]

Libet argued that consciousness is a fundamental property of nature, like the inertia of mass. "Fundamental physical phenomena," he asserted, "are not

136 Ibid., 80, 48-49, 53.

137 Ibid., 75-80.

138 Benjamin Libet, *Mind Time: The Temporal Factor in Consciousness* (Harvard University Press, 2004), 11, 197.

139 Michael Egnor, "Does Science Disprove Free Will? A Physicist Says No," *Mind Matters*, Nov 22, 2021, https://mindmatters.ai/2021/11/does-science-disprove-free-will-a-physicist-says-no/.

reducible or explainable. We simply accept these as 'given' in the nature of things. We can only study how these manifestations affect, interact, and control what goes on in the physical world."[140]

Founders of quantum physics argued early in the twentieth century that consciousness is fundamental and cannot be explained away as the product of brains. Max Planck (1858-1947) wrote, "I regard matter as derivative from consciousness. We cannot get behind consciousness."[141] Physicist Erwin Schrödinger (1887-1961) affirmed, "Consciousness is a singular that has no plural. Mind is always now. There is really no before and after for the mind."[142] Schrödinger added, "This life of yours which you are living is not merely a piece of the entire existence, but is, in a certain sense, the whole; only this whole is not so constituted that it can be surveyed in one glance."[143]

Nonetheless, neuroscientist and Nobel laureate Francis Crick (1916-2004) argued forcefully for the materialist and reductionistic view of the brain, which continues to be accepted by most scientists and also many philosophers. Crick asserted that, "a person's mental activities are entirely due to the behavior of nerve cells, glial cells, and the atoms, ions, and molecules that make up and influence them."[144]

English astronomer David Darling, however, concurs with Libet, Planck, and Schrödinger, that our consciousness is not simply a product of brain activity. In his 1995 book *Soul Search: A Scientist Explores the Afterlife*, Darling suggests a brain functions like "a reducing valve" that "shields us from an awareness of every little thing, letting through only those experiences that are relevant to our survival." The brain's role in managing perception is to screen out less critical sensory experience and focus on what is most relevant for our next action. By receiving and organizing input, however, the brain becomes "the barrier that stands between us and the limitless potential of the universe."

Darling offers a clarifying scientific critique of the materialist and reductionistic view of consciousness. "Science starts from the assumption that there is a knowable logic to the universe—which there clearly is. It then strips away all aspects of the world that logic cannot tease apart, calling these subjective.

140 Benjamin Libet, *Mind Time*, 141, 146-147, 153, 163, 173.

141 Big Think, Dec. 22, 2014, https://bigthink.com/words-of-wisdom/max-planck-i-regard-consciousness-as-fundamental.

142 Deepak Chopra, *The Future of God: A Practical Approach to Spirituality for Our Times* (Harmony Books, 2014), 133-134.

143 Deepak Chopra, *Quantum Healing*, xviii.

144 Larry Dossey, *One Mind: How Our Individual Mind Is Part of a Greater Consciousness and Why It Matters* (Hay House, 2013), 271.

There is nothing wrong with this—science couldn't progress in any other way. The mistake is to assume that this separation of objective from subjective, which *we* choose to make, reflects how things really are."

He argues, "Consciousness is not some side-effect, or epiphenomenon, of the objective world." On the contrary, "It is an integral, irreducible part of reality. Consciousness *is* the subjective aspect of all things—the ever-present *mind* of the universe."[145]

Today, almost all scientists acknowledge that our minds affect matter. Cognitive scientist Evan Thompson in his 2010 book, *Mind in Life: Biology, Phenomenology, and the Sciences of Mind*, asserts, "The world is never given to us as a brute fact detachable from our conceptual frameworks. Rather, it shows up in all the describable ways it does thanks to the structure of our subjectivity and our intentional activities."[146]

Physicist Freeman Dyson (1923-2020) affirmed, "We can recognize *informational* causality as something qualitatively distinct from physical causality, coexisting with the latter and just as efficacious. Roughly speaking, whereas in classical physics the determination of force by force requires a flow of energy, from the standpoint of information theory the determination of form by form requires a flow of information."[147]

Neuroscientist Mario Beauregard and journalist Denyse O'Leary explain in their 2008 book, *The Spiritual Brain: A Neuroscientist's Case for the Existence of the Soul*: "Through us, evolution becomes conscious, that is, driven not simply by drives for survival and reproduction but more by complex sets of insights, goals, desires, and beliefs."[148]

Philosopher John Dewey (1859-1952) describes "the mind not merely as a network property of interacting cranial neurons but rather as being equally dependent on the interactions among a brain, a nervous system, a body, and a world."[149] He envisioned the mind as an integrating process of both subjective and objective experience. Similarly, philosopher Alva Noë argues that we are

---

145 David Darling, *Soul Search: A Scientist Explores the Afterlife* (Villard Books, 1995), 158, 161.

146 Evan Thompson, *Mind in Life: Biology, Phenomenology, and the Sciences of Mind* (Belknap Press: An Imprint of Harvard University Press, 2010), 82.

147 Paul Davies, *The Cosmic Blueprint: New Discoveries in Nature's Creative Ability to Order the Universe* (Templeton Press, 2004), 190.

148 Mario Beauregard and Denyse O'Leary, *The Spiritual Brain: A Neuroscientist's Case for the Existence of the Soul* (HarperOne, 2008), 152.

149 Teed W. Rockwell, *Neither Brain Nor Ghost: A Nondualist Alternative to the Mind-Brain Identity Theory* (Bradford Book, 2007), xi.

not our brains. "The conscious mind is not inside us," he writes, but is an "active attunement to the world, an achieved integration. It is the world itself, all around, that fixes the nature of conscious experience."[150]

In *Transcendent Mind: Rethinking the Science of Consciousness*, published in 2016 by the American Psychological Association, authors Imants Barušs and Julia Mossbridge, declare, "We are in the midst of a sea change. Receding from view is materialism, whereby physical phenomena are assumed to be primary, and consciousness is regarded as secondary. Approaching is a complete reversal of perspective. According to this alternative view, consciousness is primary, and the physical is secondary."[151]

Viewing consciousness scientifically as primary enables a much richer conversation involving Hindu and Buddhist insights, as well as indigenous and other spiritual traditions. Consciousness remains a mystery, but now attempts to model consciousness become more credible and inclusive.

Deepak Chopra's training in medicine and meditation enables him to combine scientific and Hindu insights in his assessment of consciousness. He suggests: "A model that is at the same time extremely ancient and extremely modern. It is a model that says that the human body is not an anatomical structure that is fixed in space and time. The human body is more like a river alive with energy, information, and intelligence. It has a cybernetic feedback loop and can influence its own evolution and its own expression. It has the ability to learn from mistakes and the ability to make choices." Yet, "the reality is you cannot step into the same flesh and bones twice, just as you cannot step into the same river twice, because in every moment of your existence you are renewing your body more easily, more effortlessly, and more spontaneously than you can even change your clothes."

Chopra points out that in every breath we inhale 10^{22} atoms from the universe and exhale the same number of atoms from all our internal organs. Despite knowing that atoms are mostly empty space, many people may not appreciate the consequence that the human body is 99.999% empty space! And so is the universe as a whole!

He asks, "Is this nothingness just a void, or could it be the womb of creation? Is it even vaguely possible that nature goes to exactly the same place to

---

150 Alva Noë, *Out of Our Heads: Why You Are Not Your Brain and Other Lessons from the Biology of Consciousness* (Hill and Wang, 2009), 141.

151 Imants Barušs and Julia Mossbridge, *Transcendent Mind: Rethinking the Science of Consciousness* (American Psychological Association, 2016).

create a galaxy of stars, or a rain forest, or a human body, as it goes to create a thought? Because what is a thought, after all, if not a fluctuation of energy and information?"

Hindu philosophy formulated as Vedic science says Mind is one—a field of infinite possibilities. Yet, mind is also many, "because even though it has infinite choices available to it in every moment of its existence, it is not making the same choices." In Hindu teaching, Chopra asserts, what science now identifies as "the unified field—the potentiality of the forces of nature that transform themselves into material events—is nothing other than consciousness itself."

Using an image that physicist David Bohm (1917-1992) suggested, Chopra affirms: "The ultimate implicate order unfolds into the explicate order of space/time events; and there is one seamless wholeness underneath all of this where we are part of a web—a cosmic web—that is inseparably interconnected with every one of its components."[152]

In the Hindu worldview, material reality is ephemeral; thus, the material reality that humans experience actually hides reality. I suggest that Bohm's concept of an implicate order is a way of referring to a spiritual reality that is primary but hidden from us, yet also may appear within material reality.

Buddhist philosophy and practice also offer ways to awaken from the illusions of material life. The Dalai Lama in *The Universe in a Single Atom* asserts that science and Buddhist methods of exploring reality involve empirical research as well as reasoning. Yet, when Buddhist teaching refers to empirical experience, it has a broader view including "meditative states as well as the evidence of the senses." Buddhist discourse "encompasses the subjective world of experience as well as the question of values."

As most Western scientists do not study psychic experiences, the Dalai Lama suggests that Western psychology may be missing the "recognition of a specific faculty that apprehends mental phenomena. Such phenomena include a wide array of cognitive experiences, such as memory and recollection, which are, from the Buddhist point of view, qualitatively different from sensory experience."

Buddhist psychology does not separate cognitive and emotional states as in Western psychology and is more concerned with clarifying "afflictive and

---

152 Deepak Chopra, "Quantum Physics and Consciousness," in Karen Nesbitt Shanor, ed., *The Emerging Mind* (Renaissance Books, 1999), 111-12, 114, 125-26, 128. The image of an implicate order unfolding an explicate order is explained in David Bohm's 1980 book, *Wholeness and the Implicate Order*.

non-afflictive mental states" in order to cultivate and teach effective methods of meditation. The goal of Buddhist teaching is to help individuals realize "ethical well-being," not only for themselves but also for others.[153]

Hindus offer liberation from the illusions of materiality by accepting and transcending the ephemeral nature of the ordinary reality we experience. Buddhists train the mind (and the body) to replace afflictive emotions with non-afflictive emotions. Each discipline offers liberation from the cycle of rebirth, but Buddhists teach this can be realized within a single material lifetime through meditative practice.

The Dalai Lama sponsors dialogue with scientists because he believes spirituality and science are complementary approaches and share the goal of seeking truth. He hopes that Buddhists and others practicing spiritual disciplines may, in dialogue with scientists, "be of better service to the needs and well-being of humanity."[154]

Physician Larry Dossey, author of the 2013 book *One Mind: How Our Individual Mind Is Part of a Greater Consciousness and Why It Matters*, offers this story to illustrate the power of a greater consciousness. Mellen-Thomas Benedict, who in 1982 was dying from an inoperable brain tumor, declined chemotherapy, because he wanted to experience fully his death. He spent 18 months in hospice care before waking up one morning with the knowledge that he would die that day. His hospice nurse agreed not to move his dead body for at least six hours after his death, so he could experience anything that might happen after he stopped breathing.

Soon he experienced being outside his body and seeing a wondrous light. "I just went into it," he said later, "the kind of light that heals."

He felt his negative feelings about others being replaced with a more loving attitude and conversed with "the Great Light" while riding on a "stream of consciousness through the galaxy." He discovered that there is no death, only immortality, and with this realization the entire process reversed and he returned to his body.

When his hospice nurse entered his room, she was unable to detect any signs of life. To honor her agreement with Benedict, she left the body on the bed. Later Benedict was surprised to find himself awake. He tried to get out of bed but fell to the floor. When the nurse heard sounds from his room, she entered and found him alive but too weak to stand.

---

153 Dalai Lama, *The Universe in a Single Atom*, 31-35,134,146-48,169-70, 176-79.

154 Ibid., 4.

Three days later Benedict was well enough to be discharged from hospice care. After three months, a friend suggested he be tested again for his tumor. Upon reviewing the new scans, his physician confirmed that the tumor was gone. Benedict affirmed it was a miracle. The physician disagreed, calling his recovery "spontaneous remission."[155]

Dossey quotes "a neurologist at a leading medical school," who not only argues that near-death experiences are simply produced by our brains but condemns those who claim otherwise. "People like to say that these experiences are proof that consciousness can exist outside the brain, like a soul that lives after death. I hope that is true, but it is a matter of faith; there is no evidence. People who claim otherwise are using false science to engender false hope, and I think that is misleading and ultimately cruel."[156]

Scientists included in this book, however, assert that consciousness transcends brain activity as well as brain death. Physicians Alexander, Amatuzio, Anderson, Dossey, Kübler-Ross, Morse, Parti, and Jung as well as psychiatrists Fenwick, Greyson, and Moody support sharing the evidence for an afterlife with dying patients. Jung writes: "I made every effort to strengthen the belief in immortality, especially with older patients when such questions come threateningly close." Jung argues, "seen in correct psychological perspective, death is not an end but a goal."[157]

Alexander says: "To me one thing that has emerged from my experience and from very rigorous analysis of that experience over several years, talking it over with others that I respect in neuroscience, and really trying to come up with an answer, is that consciousness outside of the brain is a fact. It's an established fact. And of course, that was hard for me to accept, for I'd been a card-toting reductive materialist for decades."[158]

Peter and Elizabeth Fenwick, on the basis of their research with near-death survivors, propose that "during the dying process mind and brain separate." They suggest that mind enters "a phase of consciousness which it interprets as light." Mind utilizes "life's memories," constructing near-death images reflecting "cultural and individual differences," forming new memories "of a quite

155 Larry Dossey, *One Mind*, 87-88.

156 Ibid, 90, in Amanda Gefter, "Near-Death Neurologist: Dreams on the Border of Life," *New Scientist*, Dec. 22, 2010; 2792:80-81.

157 Jenny Yates, ed., *Jung on Death and Immortality* (Princeton University Press, 2000), 3.

158 Eben Alexander, "He said it: A neurosurgeon confronts the non-material nature of consciousness," *Uncommon Descent*, Dec. 2, 2011, https://uncommondescent.com/intelligent-design/he-said-it-a-neurosurgeon-confronts-the-non-material-nature-of-consciousness/.

different reality." The Fenwicks also propose that perhaps, "we are able to experience this aspect of mind only when our basic cognitive model-building brain is silenced"—by meditation, or by near-death experiences, or in "moments of mystical experience."[159]

Skeptics argue that the *loss of blood flow* to the brain and *a flat EEG do not exclude activity somewhere* in the brain that might account for the memories of near-death survivors. In his book, *Consciousness Beyond Life*, however, van Lommel responds: "The issue is not whether there is some immeasurable activity somewhere but whether there is any sign of those specific forms of brain activity that, according to current neuroscience, are considered essential to experiencing consciousness."

Van Lommel concludes, much as Penfield and the Fenwicks have, that there is a separation of mind and brain. "On the strength of the prospective studies of near-death experience and recent data from neurophysiological research and concepts of quantum theory, [consciousness] cannot be localized in any particular place—not even in the brain." Van Lommel also reminds us that because "the body restricts our ability to *perceive true reality*, this true reality is by definition unknowable."[160]

The evidence of what Alexander and Anderson call "heaven" or what van Lommel calls "endless consciousness" or what Hawkes identifies as "the Source" and Jackson "the Other Side" is based on personal experience. Yet, careful research conducted by many other physicians and researchers also verifies that patients have had conscious experiences and memories when their brains were measurably incapable of producing either.

Physicists Paul Davies and John Gribbin propose that quantum field theory may help us understand consciousness. "Even the apparent solidity of ordinary matter melts away into a frolic of insubstantial patterns of energy."[161] Reality at this smallest of levels involves "an interlocking network of information exchange—a holistic, indeterministic and open system—vibrant with potentialities and bestowed with infinite richness."

Davies and Gribbin suggest that, "The human mind is a by-product of this vast informational process, a by-product with the curious capability of being able to *understand*, at least in part, the principles on which the process runs."[162]

---

159 Peter and Elizabeth Fenwick, *The Truth in the Light*, 259, 265.

160 Pim van Lommel, *Consciousness Beyond Life*, 260, 285.

161 Paul Davies and John Gribbin, *The Matter Myth: Dramatic Discoveries that Challenge Our Understanding of Physical Reality* (Simon & Schuster, 2006), 235.

162 Ibid., 308-309.

Physicist Michio Kaku acknowledges that memory "might not be entirely neural," as "memories are not linked spatially [in the brain] but rather temporally, by vibrating in unison." He suggests that memory involves an information flow "in the form of resonance *across* brain structures."[163] If memory does involve *resonance* that is not simply a product of billions of brain neurons, this might explain how a man could have an IQ of 126 even though a brain scan revealed his cerebral cortex was less than one-eighth inch thick and "95 percent of his skull was filled with cerebrospinal fluid."[164]

Memory involving *resonance* would need an information field. Physicist Peter Russell reminds us that our thoughts "are not material things; they are not made of atoms or anything physical. Yet our thoughts clearly exist." In our experience, he notes, "The scenes or sounds that constitute a memory are all 'in the mind,' and are likewise just modulations in [what he calls] the *field of knowing*. Similarly, when we imagine the future, we may experience images, sounds, smells, tastes, or feelings. These too are just arising in me. They are appearing in the same *field of knowing* in which my thoughts are appearing."[165]

From his research on human subjectivity, Libet concluded that what we call the "self" and the "soul" are contents of our mental awareness that are as real as our physical neurons and organs. "Soulful feelings are especially important" and are "expressed in music, art, literature, and, of course, religious and spiritual activities. Such phenomenal feelings should not be dismissed lightly, without convincing counter evidence," Libet affirmed. "Our subjective inner life is what really matters to us as human beings."[166]

"When it comes to the mental realm," Davies agrees "the characteristic qualities are even more distinctive and totally unlike anything else found in nature. Now we are dealing with thoughts, purposes, feelings, beliefs—the inner, subjective world of an observer, who experiences external reality through the senses." These experiences "do not even exist on the same level of description as material objects and bear no obvious relationship to them whatsoever." Explaining these "qualia" is "the hard problem" of consciousness, as conceptually and scientifically "these experiences are disconnected from the world of material objects and forces."[167]

---

163 Michio Kaku, *The Future of the Mind: The Scientific Quest to Understand, Enhance, and Empower the Mind* (Doubleday, 2014), 108. Italics added.

164 R. Lewin, "Is Your Brain Really Necessary?" *Science* 210 (1980): 1232-34 in Pim van Lommel, *Consciousness Beyond Death*, 197.

165 Peter Russell, "Ripples of Knowing," http://www.peterrussell.com/SP/conscrising.php. Accessed October 2, 2017.

166 Benjamin Libet, *Mind Time*, 214, 221.

167 Paul Davies, *The Goldilocks Enigma*: 228.

Philosopher Michael Grosso explains Jung's view of conscious and unconscious subjectivity in a 2017 book entitled *The Final Choice*. Grosso writes: "What is real, effective, and fateful is the psyche. We are immersed in a sea of deep collective images, linked somehow to vital and cosmic forces. These exist as the living forms of internal existence; what is more, as Jung believed, they are both 'subjective' and 'objective.'" For Jung, "What is deeply within leads to what is deeply without."[168] Unconscious subjective experience manifests in conscious objective events.

Jung proposed a model of the "collective unconscious" after discovering in his patients' dreams, "mythological motifs from cultures of which they had no intellectual knowledge." This led him to affirm that we all participate in and are affected by an unconscious level of human history and culture.[169]

Jung had dinner with Einstein several times and wrote in a 1953 letter that Einstein started him thinking about how the relativity of time and space verified by physicists affects the psyche. In an essay entitled "The Soul and Death," Jung asserts that, "We are not entitled to conclude from the apparent space-time quality of our perception that there is no form of existence without space and time." Jung suggested that the psyche, in its depth, "participates in an existence beyond space and time" and "partakes of what is inadequately and symbolically described as *eternity*."[170]

In their 2017 book, *You are the Universe*, Chopra and physicist Menas C. Kafatos write "we live in an unbounded state of consciousness that we call the universe." They argue, "Reality consists of shifting, interchangeable states that emanate from one source: consciousness," which "is continuous and present in everything."

We can see that "the universe is behaving, not like bits of matter colliding but like a mind doing everything with a purpose." We don't need "to meet and greet a cosmic architect." Quantum physics has revealed that "the universe is one undivided whole" and its parts, "whether we are talking about atoms, galaxies, or forces like gravity, are just qualia—the qualities of consciousness."

---

168 Michael Grosso, *The Final Choice: Playing the Survival Game* (Stillpoint Publishing, 1985), 125-26.

169 Stanislav Grof, "The Revision and Re-Enchantment of Psychology: The Legacy of Half a Century of Consciousness Research," https://galileocommission.org/revision-and-re-enchantment-of-psychology-legacy-of-half-a-century-of-consciousness-research-grof-2012/.

170 Jenny Yates, *Jung On Death and Immortality,* 4-5.

"Qualia refers to how we experience life rather than how we measure it." Unlike quanta, the plural of quantum, which "are 'packets' of energy, qualia are the everyday qualities of existence—light, sound, color, shape, texture." Chopra and Kafatos assert that, "Qualia are the true building blocks of reality."

Because "qualia are *subjective*, they directly attack the objectivity of modern science. Moreover, because experience is *meaningful*, qualia attack the model of random, meaningless nature." It is qualia that "allow us to connect everything together through a common property—every single thing is an aspect of one field of consciousness."[171]

Cognitive scientist Donald D. Hoffman in his 2020 book, *The Case Against Reality: Why Evolution Hid the Truth from Our Eyes*, reaffirms with Chopra and Kafatos, as well as Planck, Schrödinger, and Libet, that consciousness is fundamental. "There is a screen—an interface—between us and objective reality," Hoffman asserts. "Can we hope to pierce that screen and see objective reality?" He answers affirmatively, by proposing a model of reality that he identifies as *conscious realism*. Hoffman explains, "We have met reality and it is like us. We are conscious agents, and so is objective reality."

In other words, Hoffman argues that all we can know about what is real is framed by our subjective conscious experience. This also means, however, that because we know a conscious agent cannot "describe itself completely," every conscious agent remains "at least in part, unconscious to itself."[172]

As a physicist, Thomas Campbell was asked by businessman Robert Monroe (1915-1995) to help him research the out-of-body experiences he was having and wanted to study more scientifically. Monroe published several books about his experiences and founded the Monroe Institute to support consciousness research.[173]

Campbell also began to explore consciousness using Monroe's method of inducing out-of-body experiences. In his 2003 book, *My Big TOE (Theory of Everything): A Trilogy Unifying Philosophy, Physics, and Metaphysics*, Campbell describes a model of reality based both on his personal out-of-body journeys in the cosmos and his scientific research and reasoning.

"We are participants in an evolving consciousness ecosystem," Campbell argues, "that includes and transcends our experience within the universe." Each and every sentient being is "a limited implementation of consciousness"

---

171 Chopra and Kafatos, *You are the Universe: Discovering Your Cosmic Self and Why It Matters* (Harmony Books, 2017), 149, 224, 229-230, 239, 241, 213-215, 250.

172 David D. Hoffman, *The Case Against Reality: Why Evolution Hid the Truth from Our Eyes* (2020, W. W. Norton & Company. Kindle Edition), 175-178,180-181.

173 https://www.monroeinstitute.org/.

created "to serve a particular evolutionary purpose (occupy an available niche) within the greater consciousness ecosystem." Our physical universe, Campbell asserts, "is a small virtual habitat" in this larger evolving mental ecosystem.

To the reader he writes, "You have been designed primarily to evolve the quality of your being—the quality of your consciousness." It should be clear to all of us, he asserts, that, "Growing up within a larger reality has much more to do with raising the quality of our consciousness than with accumulating information."

The origin of consciousness remains a mystery, but as conscious beings we have significant choices. "What matters most," Campbell affirms, "is the development of wisdom, understanding, and the capacity to love."[174]

174 Thomas Campbell, *My Big TOE [Theory of Everything]: A Trilogy Unifying Philosophy, Physics, and Metaphysics* (Lightning Strikes Books, 2003), 221, 250, 299, 354, 567, 741. See 637: "The data upon which this model is based represent my best **objective** evaluation of my **subjective** experience."

Purpose and Meaning

Many scientists have viewed the evolving world as the result of random gene mutations and changing environmental conditions. Biologist and Nobel Prize winner Jacques Monod's 1970 book, *Chance and Necessity: Essay on the Natural Philosophy of Modern Biology*, asserts this view and is often cited by other scientists. Those who share this belief reject any argument for an objective purpose in the universe, allowing only the subjective purposes of humans and perhaps other creatures with some measure of consciousness.

Mathematician and philosopher Alfred North Whitehead (1861-1947) noted the irony of this reasoning: "Many a scientist, has patiently designed experiments for the *purpose* of substantiating his belief that animal operations are motivated by no purposes. He has perhaps spent his spare time in writing articles to prove that human beings are as other animals so that *purpose* is a category irrelevant for the explanation of their bodily activities, his own activities included. Scientists animated by the purpose of proving that they are purposeless," he concludes, "constitute an interesting subject for study."[175]

In Goff's book, *Why? The Purpose of the Universe*, he acknowledges that most scientists agree there is no measurable evidence of a purpose for the universe. Yet, there is considerable scientific evidence of what is called the "fine-tuning" of the universe, verifying how extremely improbable the universe actually is. Goff reasons, "If the evidence is more likely assuming the theory is true than it is assuming the theory is false, then the evidence supports the theory."

For example, Goff explains: "The strong nuclear force—the force that binds together the elements in the nucleus of the atom—can be represented by the number 0.007. If that value had been 0.006 or less the universe would have contained nothing but hydrogen: the simplest element. If it had been 0.008 or higher, almost all of the hydrogen would have been burned off in the Big Bang and water would never have existed. In either case, there would be none of the chemical complexity we find in our universe."[176]

175 Alfred North Whitehead, Process and Reality, 15-16, in Edward Kelly and Emily Kelly, *Irreducible Mind: Toward a Psychology for the 21st Century* (Rowman & Littlefield, 2009), 641.

176 Phillip Goff, *Why?*, 48-50, 35-36.

Paleoanthropologist Bernard Wood reminds us that in the scientific method, "Absence of evidence is not evidence of absence."[177] He is referring to anthropological efforts to construct the human evolutionary story, but this principle applies to all scientific efforts to tell the history of the universe. The absence of evidence explaining *why* something happened does not justify concluding that there is no reason for why it happened.

Physicist Paul Davies asserts that he belongs to a "dissenting minority" of scientists who "maintain that life is not merely an incidental by-product of nature but a deeply significant part of the cosmic story." He writes, "I do believe that life and mind are etched deeply into the fabric of the cosmos, perhaps through a shadowy, half-glimpsed life principle; and if I am to be honest, I have to concede that this starting point is something I feel more in my heart than in my head."

In *The Goldilocks Enigma: Why is the Universe Just Right for Life?* Davies argues the odds against a random chance explanation for the universe are enormous. Also, if we rely on Donald Hoffman's conclusion that the nature of the universe is present in our knowledge of ourselves as conscious beings, isn't it reasonable to argue that our experience of purpose and meaning is evidence that the cosmos, too, has purpose and meaning?

Davies quotes other scientists who affirm that reality has purpose and meaning. Physicist Freeman Dyson (1923-2020) asserted, "As we look out into the universe and identify the many accidents of physics and astronomy that have worked together to our benefit, it almost seems as if the universe must, in some sense, have known we were coming." Biologist Simon Conway Morris proposes, "There is, if you like, seeded into the initiation of the universe itself the inevitability of intelligence." Nobel Prize-winning biologist Christian de Duve describes the universe as "pregnant with life" and calls life "a cosmic imperative." Stuart Kauffman declares that humanity is "at home in the universe." [178]

Our answer, of course, depends on how we describe nature. E. O. Wilson (1929-2021) in his 1999 book, *Consilience: The Unity of Knowledge*, asks, "What is human nature?" He answers: "It is not the genes, which prescribe it, or culture, its ultimate product. Rather, human nature is something else for which we have only begun to find ready expression. It is the epigenetic rules, the hereditary regularities of mental development that bias cultural evolution in one direction as opposed to another, and thus connect the genes to culture."

---

177 Michael Greshko, "These Early Humans Lived 300,000 Years Ago—But Had Modern Faces," N*ational Geographic*, June 7, 2017, https://www.nationalgeographic.com/news/2017/06/morocco-early-human-fossils-anthropology-science/.

178 Paul Davies, *The Goldilocks Enigma*, 222-223, 280.

Epigenetic rules, Wilson asserts, "are innate operations in the sensory system and brain. They are rules of thumb that allow organisms to find rapid solutions to problems encountered in the environment. They predispose individuals to view the world in a particular innate way and automatically to make certain choices as opposed to others. With epigenetic rules, we see a rainbow in four basic colors and not in a continuum of light frequencies. We avoid mating with a sibling, speak in grammatically coherent sentences, smile at friends, and when alone fear strangers in first encounters."[179]

Ethics, too, Wilson argues may be explained as the result of epigenetic rules: "By moral sentiments is now meant moral instincts as defined by the modern behavioral sciences, subject to judgment according to their consequences. The sentiments are thus derived from epigenetic rules, hereditary biases in mental development, usually conditioned by emotion, that influence concepts and decisions made from them."[180]

In *Consilience* Wilson criticizes anthropologists who, because of their "humanitarian purpose," have supported cultural relativism, which Wilson argues has undermined the biological fact that human nature is rooted in our epigenetic rules. "There is a hereditary selective advantage to membership in a powerful group united by devout belief and purpose. Even when individuals subordinate themselves and risk death in a common cause, their genes are more likely to be transmitted to the next generation than are those of competing groups who lack equivalent resolve."[181]

In summary, Wilson claims that epigenetic rules have generated the human experience of purpose as a way of ensuring survival of our genes. Values, too, he argues, such as art, loyalty to one's tribal group, and the altruism that loyalty may require in sacrificing oneself for one's group, have contributed to the survival of our species. Wilson urges that scholars unite all the disciplines of knowledge in support of this biological view of human nature, encoded by evolution in our epigenetic rules.

In contrast, biologists Robert Rosen (1934-1998) and A. H. Louie address questions about human purpose on the basis of "relational biology." Rosen agrees with Wilson that all disciplines of knowledge should base their predictions on a scientific theory. "To one degree or another," Rosen argues, "this 'question of ought' is the same question the biologists, the economists, the political scientists, the urban planners, the futurists, and many others want to

179 E. O. Wilson, *Consilience: The Unity of Knowledge* (Vintage Books, 1999), 171-210.
180 Ibid., 233, 275.
181 Ibid., 201, 282.

know." All knowledge "is in effect a technology of decision-making. But underlying any technology there must be an underlying foundation of basic principles: a science, a *theory*."

Advocates of relational biology do not agree with Wilson. Instead, they support a "theory of anticipatory systems." Rosen writes, "An anticipatory system is a natural system that contains an internal predictive model of itself and of its environment, which allows it to change state at an instant in accord with the model's predictions pertaining to a later instant."

In this biological theory, "The presence of a predictive model serves to pull the future into the present; a system with a *good* model thus behaves in many ways as if it can anticipate the future."

Louie argues that scientists have resisted a theory of "anticipation" because the dominant scientific paradigm assumes:

> "The essential basis on which *genuine scientific inquiry* rests is the principle of causality (which an anticipatory system seems to violate).
>
> And *true objective science* cannot be argued from final cause (but an anticipatory system seems to embody a form of teleology)."

The dominant scientific paradigm assumes causality is entirely due to past events that may be objectively confirmed as affecting subsequent events. It rejects any claim that biological activity is purposeful (teleological).

Relational biology, however, recognizes, "There must be information about self, about species, and about the evolutionary environment, encoded into the organization of all living systems." Louie adds: "Biology is replete with situations in which organisms can generate and maintain internal predictive models of themselves and their environments and use the predictions of these models about the future for the purpose of control in the present. Much, if not most, biological behavior is model-based in this sense. This is true at every level, from the molecular to the cellular to the physiological to the behavioral, and this is true in all parts of the biosphere, from microbes to plants to animals to ecosystems."[182]

For scientists who defend neo-Darwinian evolutionary explanations, purpose only arises in human culture to enable species survival. For Rosen, Louie, and other dynamic system scientists, purposeful actions employing anticipatory models guide all living organisms, and therefore reflect a fundamental fact

182 A. H. Louie, "Robert Rosen's Anticipatory Systems," January 2010, https://www.researchgate.net/publication/228091658_Robert_Rosen's_anticipatory_systems.

about reality as manifested in the life on this planet. *Not only humans, but all creatures create anticipatory models enabling them to respond to challenging circumstances that arise.*

Anticipatory reasoning, for humans, becomes a major preoccupation. Thomas Nagel, in his 2012 book *Mind and Cosmos: Why the Materialist Neo-Darwinian Conception of Nature is Almost Certainly False*, asserts that, "An adequate conception of the cosmos must contain the resources to account for how it could have given rise to beings capable of thinking successfully about what is good and bad, right and wrong, and discovering moral and evaluative truths that do not depend on their own beliefs."

Nagel argues, "Value enters the world with life, and the capacity to recognize and be influenced by value in its large extension appears with higher forms of life." This means, "Value is not just an accidental side effect of life; rather, there is value because life is a necessary condition of value."[183] Anticipatory systems that have evolved are a form of valuing.

Physicist David Deutsch argues in his 2012 book, *The Beginning of Infinity: Explanations that Transform the World*, that humans learn to understand information not simply to survive but to be creative. "Of all the countless biological adaptations that have evolved on our planet," Deutsch asserts, "*creativity* is the only one that can produce scientific or mathematical knowledge, art or philosophy."[184]

Deutsch contrasts "explanatory" and "non-explanatory" knowledge. Genetic and epigenetic rules illustrate the non-explanatory knowledge that is utilized efficiently within our bodies and is largely unconscious. Only explanatory knowledge, Deutsch suggests, has the ability to solve problems "beyond those that they were created to solve." Only explanatory knowledge uses "conjectures" for the purpose of thinking creatively.[185]

"The reach of ideas into the world of abstractions," Deutsch writes, "is a property of the knowledge that they contain, not of the brain in which they may happen to be instantiated." In fact, "There is a kind of infinite reach that is unique to people: the reach of the ability to understand explanations." Persons, Deutsch reminds us, "Consist of abstract information, including the distinctive

183 Thomas Nagel, *Mind and Cosmos: Why the Materialist Neo-Darwinian Conception of Nature is Almost Certainly False* (Oxford University Press, 2012), 84-86, 105, 121-123.

184 David Deutsch, *The Beginning of Infinity*, 398, 409-410.

185 Ibid., 30, 78-79.

ideas, theories, intentions, feelings and other states of mind that characterize an 'I'." Our intentions are based on abstract information, but nonetheless "are real and can play a role in causing physical phenomena."[186]

Physicist Jim Baggott, author of the 2013 book *Farewell to Reality: How Modern Physics Has Betrayed the Search for Scientific Truth*, sums up the scientific understanding of explanatory knowledge in what is sometimes called *The Veracity Principle*. "It is not possible to verify a scientific theory such that it provides absolute certainty for all time. A theory is instead accepted (or even tolerated), on the basis of its ability to survive the tests and meet additional criteria of simplicity, efficacy, utility, explanatory power and less rational, innately human measures such as beauty."[187]

As uniquely creative humans, we may discover beauty in the creativity of the universe. Also, with beauty as a measure of scientific veracity, we are able to experience and appreciate that magnificence of an evolving universe that continues to be creative amidst colossal disorder.

Journey of the Universe, a video and book created by mathematician Brian Thomas Swimme and Confucian scholar Mary Evelyn Tucker, embraces the spiritual dimension of the universe. Stars are physically material objects but have a "life" of their own. For stars have created all the elements in the universe from the hydrogen and helium existing after the origin of the universe. *The Journey of the Universe* suggests that, "The stars are our ancestors. Out of them, everything comes forth."[188]

Incredibly, "We are living in a universe that is expanding at just the rate necessary for life to emerge."[189] Billions of years were required for stars to form, create heavier elements including carbon from hydrogen and helium, explode to seed the cosmos, and then for this dust to create planets and here in this solar system create life. Time was needed for consciousness, value, and explanatory knowledge to be embodied—in a species that could tell its story as well as its version of the creative story of the universe.

Chopra and Kafatos in their book *You Are the Universe* assert: "It's an axiom in science that the relevant questions are about *how*, not *why*." Nevertheless, "The evolution of life keeps bringing up issues of *why*."

---

186 Ibid., 123-124, 130.

187 Jim Baggott, *Farewell to Reality: How Modern Physics Has Betrayed the Search for Scientific Truth* (Pegasus Books, 2014), 22

188 Brian Thomas Swimme and Mary Evelyn Tucker, *The Journey of the Universe* (Yale University Press, 2011), 29 and 120.

189 Ibid., 10-11.

"In a conscious universe, everything is alive. The observation that life comes from life turns out to be a cosmic truth. And we can see this in quantum physics, for quantum particles 'behave in a totally lifelike way (i.e., making choices, balancing stability and spontaneity, efficiently harvesting energy, and so on).'"

They conclude, "A universe is defined by the creatures who inhabit it." This is not only true for humans but for all creatures on earth and any creatures anywhere.

"Why is the human mind creative?

Because the cosmos is creative.

Why did the human mind evolve?

Because evolution is built into the fabric of reality itself.

Why do our lives have meaning?

Because nature proceeds with a drive toward purpose and truth."[190]

Brian Thomas Swimme's 2022 book, *Cosmogenesis*, includes several striking affirmations by cultural historian Thomas Berry (1914-2009), who asserts, "The universe created humans."

In the evolution of humans on this planet, carbon atoms are an integral component of the embodiment of consciousness within physical forms. Stars create carbon. "Did the universe ask us to pay for this? No. Have we done anything that merits this cosmic gift? No." As "unmerited love" is what we mean by *grace*—"love freely given"—Berry affirms the exploding stars in the universe "are bestowers of grace."

"While it is true," Berry admits, "that our ancestral stars did not know they were giving birth to us, it is wrong to say stars do not know. They do know. They know how to create carbon, silver, boron, and calcium."

These are the stars that became large enough and hot enough to create the heavier elements. Scientists call them *supernovas*. Berry affirms, "The central revelation of the supernova is its irreversible gift-giving. Irreversible because the star uses its energy to fashion the elements, and once that energy is used, it is not restored. The giving requires the star's death."

---

190 Deepak Chopra and Menas Kafatos, *You Are the Universe*, 178-179, 183, 198, 207, 215, 217-218, 221-222, 229, 248. Bold font added.

"Scientists estimate," Berry reports, "that with the passing of each second another star has exploded and is disbursing its treasures. This extravagant gift-giving," Berry affirms, "is the *spirituality* of the universe." It is a form of cosmic love that enables the future to emerge.

"Our ancient epics extol humans who give their lives for the wellbeing of the community. Even if these authors knew nothing of supernovas, they were intuitively aware that the universe values generosity. The generous personality is the human mode of a supernova's extravagant gift-giving."

Berry, a Catholic priest concludes, "What I have to offer in terms of faith is simple in the extreme. My trust is in the stars' bestowal of grace."[191]

Neurosurgeon Hamilton concludes his book, *The Scalpel and the Soul: Encounters with Surgery, the Supernatural, and Healing Power of Hope*, with this affirmation—"Creation is imbued with purpose."[192]

---

191 Brian Thomas Swimme, *Cosmogenesis* (Catapult, Kindle Edition, 2022), 293-295. Italics added.

192 Allan Hamilton, *The Scalpel and the Soul*, 216.

Nature and God

Biologist Rupert Sheldrake writes in his 1994 book, *The Rebirth of Nature: The Greening of Science and God*, "Each of us, faced with the mystery of our existence and experience, has to try to find some way of making sense of it." He identifies three worldviews that have made sense to many: "Those with the lowest mystery-tolerance thresholds are drawn to the mechanistic-atheistic worldview, which as a matter of principle denies the existence of mysterious entities like souls and God, and portrays a disenchanted, unmagical reality proceeding entirely mechanically. Those who acknowledge the life of evolutionary nature admit the mystery of life and creativity. And those who acknowledge the life of God are consciously open to the mystery of divine consciousness, grace, and love."[193]

Biologist E. O. Wilson perhaps speaks for the majority of scientists: "If humankind evolved by Darwinian natural selection, genetic change and environmental necessity, not God, made the species."[194]

The film and book *Journey of the Universe* represents the view of the universe as naturally creative, without any supernatural origin.

I have offered evidence, however, of extraordinary experiences and mysterious physical realities that cannot be explained by the mechanistic model of contemporary science or by a philosophy of naturalism. Some of these experiences support the hypothesis that there is a spiritual reality entangled with physical reality—a spiritual reality that may break into ordinary life as extraordinary knowing, and that also may be the source of all that is. Scientists who endorse this view generally refer to God as the Creator of the universe and the living earth.

Affirmations of spiritual reality expressed in this book include: the Afterlife, All That Is, Allahu Akbar, Buddha, Christ, Creator, divine Reality, endless consciousness, enhanced consciousness, Fabric of Consciousness, cosmic consciousness, God, Good, Heart of God, grace, Heaven, Highest, the life force,

---

193 Rupert Sheldrake, *The Rebirth of Nature: The Greening of Science and God* (Park Street Press, 1991, 1994), 203.

194 Kenneth R. Miller, *Finding Darwin's God: A Scientist's Search for Common Ground Between God and Evolution* (Cliff Street Books, 2007).

Light, Love, loving Presence, luminous emptiness, Mind, Maker, Om, Order of Things, the Other Side, Shechinah, Source, spiritual, supernatural, transcendent, and "unable to express in words."

Most survivors of near-death experiences, who encounter God while they feel they are dying (or dead), do not describe their extraordinary knowing by quoting scripture or affirming the teachings of a particular religious tradition. If there is a spiritual reality, it embraces stunning diversity.

As we have seen from the research and writing of many scientists, near-death survivors often report experiencing God as a bright or brilliant light accompanied by a feeling of overwhelming love. A majority of near-death survivors affirm they became more 'spiritual' because of their experience. Many of those who were religious before their near-death experience said their experience left them less likely to attend worship, as they found these rituals more dogmatic and lacking the extraordinary nature and unconditional love of their near-death experience.

Hospice physician Kircher writes of her childhood near-death experience that: "She had the strong sense that she was *surrounded* by God. She did not feel like a boy or a girl or a child or an adult. She experienced the essence of herself—the soul that had existed before she came into her body and that would exist when this life was over."

She affirmed an assurance not only of an afterlife but also of existing with God before her birth. She saw God as an aura that gave her strength and calmed her fears—not because of God's appearance but because of a feeling that she was "totally connected with God."

Parti thought of himself as a secular scientist with a Hindu background. During his near-death experience, however, he was counseled by angels and then encountered a Being of Light that called him to become a spiritual healer.

Hamilton entitled his autobiographical reflections, *The Scalpel and the Soul: Encounters with Surgery, the Supernatural, and the Healing Power of Hope*. In Africa he discovered that natives were capable of extraordinary knowing, inexplicable to him as a scientist. Hamilton's experience of a patient's ability to see and hear during her surgery, when the blood supply to her brain was shut down, convinced him that consciousness was a supernatural reality.

The near-death experience of Hawkes led her to learn and practice cell-level healing. Alexander says an affirmation from *Amazing Grace*—I was blind, but now I see—"took on new meaning, as I understood just how blind to the full nature of the spiritual universe we are on earth—especially people like I had been, who had believed that matter was the core reality, and that all else—thought, consciousness, ideas, emotions, spirit—were simply productions of it."[195]

Other scientists affirm faith in God for reasons other than having a near-death experience. Astronomer Owen Gingerich asserts, "Rather than believe that the universe is simply meaningless, a macabre joke, I would prefer to accept a universe created with intention and purpose by a loving God, and perhaps created with just enough freedom that conscience and responsibility are part of the mix." He affirms, "This belief does not interfere with the scientific enterprise," at least in his experience. Gingerich admits that the idea of a Creator is "incomprehensible" but says, "we can see the consequences of this unimaginably powerful creative act: a universe congenial to the ultimate formation of life; and life, giving rise to intelligence that can ask questions science cannot answer."[196]

Whitehead, who once thought there was no evidence of God in the natural world, "came to believe that people can and do have experiences of God." He also concluded that values and creativity in the universe could not be explained by materialist science alone. "The order of the world, the depth of reality of the world, the value of the world in its whole, and in its parts," are not an accident, Whitehead affirms, but are all bound together by "the completed ideal harmony, which is God."

For Whitehead, God is the creative lure *within* nature. Thus, in process philosophy God is not a supernatural God, but a God who brings creativity and value into each actual occasion of reality. History reveals, Whitehead asserts, that for many people this creative God within all natural events may be experienced as "the great companion—the fellow-sufferer who understands."[197]

Process philosopher and Christian theologian, John B. Cobb, Jr., believes God is, "felt by each creature in and through those possibilities relevant to that creature's unique situation." This experiencing of God "is rarely conscious even among those creatures in which consciousness occurs," but some feel a call to respond by joining a religious community. Cobb affirms: "We experience God. God experiences us. We are affected by God. God is affected by us. In God we live and move and have our being. In God nothing is lost. What is ephemeral in the world is everlasting in God."[198]

---

195 Eben Alexander, *Proof of Heaven*.

196 Owen Gingerich, *God's Universe* (Harvard University Press, 2016), 7, 96, 104.

197 David Ray Griffin, *Reenchantment without Supernaturalism: A Process Philosophy of Religion* (Cornell University Press, 2001), 88, 90-91.

198 Ibid., 409-10. See Acts 17:28 for "we live and move and have our being" in God.

Kauffman in his 2010 book, *Reinventing the Sacred: A New View of Science, Reason and Religion*, also identifies God with creativity in nature and asserts, like process philosophers and theologians, "A Creator God is not needed for the origin of life." Kauffman admits, however, that he describes nature as "sacred" because he wants to expand our understanding of what nature really is. Moreover, he explains, "That is why I feel we must use the God word, for my hope is to honorably steal its aura to authorize the sacredness of the creative in nature." Kauffman concludes his book by affirming, "May we find the creativity in nature sacred whether we are atheists or believers in a God who breathed life into this universe of ceaseless creativity."[199]

Biologist Francis Collins, who led the Human Genome Project and is head of the National Institutes of Health, describes himself as an evangelical Christian. Contrary to process thinkers, he affirms in his 2007 book, *The Language of God: A Scientist Presents Evidence for Belief*, that "God cannot be completely contained within nature." Chopra agrees. "A transcendental God permeates every spiritual tradition for a very good reason—the source of nature cannot be found by looking around at nature."[200]

For surgeon Bernie Siegel, knowing that "God is a loving, intelligent, and conscious energy" has come from dreams, drawings, and near-death experiences. He affirms: "First, there was consciousness and consciousness was with God" and "consciousness was God, because God speaks in dreams and images—the universal language."[201]

From decades of experience with patients, Siegel has learned that this eternal consciousness can be a force for healing. To a cancer patient, Siegel proposes, "Visualize God's light melting a tumor that appears as a block of ice." Siegel tells his patients, "By accepting ourselves as God's creation, seeing beauty and meaning in what we are, just as we are, we accept others as God's creation too."[202]

Near-death experiences have led many to see the afterlife as offering reincarnation in this or another world. "I have had a near-death experience," Siegel

199 Stuart A. Kauffman, *Reinventing the Sacred: A New View of Science, Reason, and Religion* (Basic Books, 2010), 2, 4, 44-45.

200 Deepak Chopra, *The Future of God*, 68.

201 I read Siegel's statement as a contemporary paraphrase of this well-known text from the New Testament, "In the beginning was the Word, and the Word was with God, and the Word was God." (John 1:1. Word is the English translation of the Greek word *Logos*, used in the ancient manuscripts of this gospel.)

202 Bernie S. Siegel and Cynthia J. Hurn, *The Art of Healing: Uncovering Your Inner Wisdom and Potential for Self-Healing* (New World Library, 2013), 198, 42, 36, 163, and 92.

confirms, "and, through this, learned that we are more than our bodies. I have had past-life experiences and messages from dead patients delivered through mediums. I have heard voices of the dead speak to me."

Instead of resisting these extraordinary experiences, Siegel embraces them as revelations verifying "a universal field," which is "the source of all creation" and "communicates with our consciousness."[203]

---

203 Ibid., 4-5 and 114.

Light and Love . . .

My father's near-death experience not only ended his fear of death but also set me on the spiritual quest I have shared with you. I have focused on the writings of scientists because their personal stories and research verify what many of them identify as a spiritual dimension of reality. Like my father, these scientists were not convinced of a spiritual reality by the teachings of one or more religious traditions, nor by any institutionalized religious practice. They were convinced by their own personal experiences or by scientific research into the inexplicable knowing of other scientists as well as nonscientists.

I am not a scientist. I have studied and taught theology, religious history, ethics, and law. I have received a Doctor of Ministry degree from the Divinity School of the University of Chicago, a Juris Doctor degree from the Dr. Martin Luther King, Jr. School of Law at the University of California at Davis, and a Ph.D. in the history of religion from the Graduate Theological School in Berkeley, California. I have taught and written about Christian faith, other religious traditions, and ethics. My most recent academic book is the third edition of *Doing Environmental Ethics*, published by Routledge in 2020.

For a decade I led an international organization of minority religious communities—in countries that had, or were now, discriminating against them. Our organization advocated for the international human right of freedom of religion or belief, and our activities always sought to model respect for the right of individuals and religious communities to affirm their religious beliefs and to participate in their rituals.[204]

My international advocacy with diverse religious leaders, who affirmed a spiritual dimension of reality, expanded my awareness and enriched my life. I recall at an interfaith gathering in Rome singing with women and men from many different religious backgrounds, "We shall overcome someday."

We affirmed our hope to overcome the fear due to religious conflicts of the past and present. We declared our resistance to the injustice inflicted on those of a different color or culture, who were and are minorities in their own

204 From 1990 to 2001 I directed the International Association for Religious Freedom (IARF) and represented it, as a consultative NGO, at the United Nations.

country. We renewed our commitment to overcome our temptation to blame others instead of striving to heal the wounds that divide religious and cultural communities having different beliefs and practices.

Singing a spiritual, which has its roots in the struggle for civil rights in the United States but is currently a global call for justice and peace, was both a thrilling and humbling experience for me. The grace I felt then has revived stirring memories of my experience as a young adult in Black churches and in civil rights marches, where with religious and nonreligious advocates for civil rights we sang the spirituals and prayed for justice.

As a civil rights worker in Mississippi in 1965, I attended Sunday worship with the Black family who hosted me in their home, and with other Black families who were striving to exercise their right to vote and to enroll their children in what were then schools only "for Whites."

Three years later, as a student at the Divinity School of the University of Chicago, I was again moved by the spirituals we sang during a demonstration for open housing on the westside of Chicago, which was led by Dr. Martin Luther King, Jr. (1929-1968) and other members of the Southern Christian Leadership Conference (SCLC).

"Oh freedom," we sang in the civil rights movement of the 1960s. "And before I'd be a slave, I'd be buried in my grave, and go home to my Lord and be free." As I recalled other spirituals that I heard and sang, suddenly hope and the promise of returning "home" rang true in me once again.

The phrase "Swing low sweet chariot," which tells of the prophet Elijah being taken up to heaven,[205] is followed by the words, "coming for to carry me home." The chorus of "Steal Away" is, "Steal away home, I ain't got long to stay here." Each verse of the spiritual, "Precious Lord," so loved by Dr. Martin Luther King, Jr., concludes with the words, "and lead me home."

John Newton, a former slave trader who became an abolitionist and a pastor, wrote the words to *Amazing Grace* that affirm, "'Tis grace has brought me safe thus far, and grace will lead me home." I've identified in this endnote the page numbers of the many near-death experiences recorded in this book, which include an affirmation of being or coming "home."[206] And now, I too, look forward to being *home* after death.

At last, I understand why my father asked that we sing *Amazing Grace* during his memorial service. After his near-death experience, I believe the words "and grace will bring me home" had new meaning for him.

205 2 Kings 2:11 in the Christian Bible.

206 Jeffrey Long, *God and the Afterlife*. The word "home" is used to refer to the afterlife on pages 11, 40, 43, 61, 66, 71, 76, 95, 103, 140, and 141.

Berman's feeling of being *home* during his mystical experience now also makes sense. As do the many reports from near-death survivors who found themselves, in the experience of a divine light, finally back *home*. Here are three published in Jeffrey Long's book, *God and the Afterlife*.

Anna: "The light sensed and felt everything, thought and understood everything; it knew I was finally back home! The light was God."

Andy: "The Light knows me, knows my name! Surrounding this Light form are millions of other lights welcoming me back home. I tell them, *It's good to be back home*. I know we're all home together again."

Sandy: "I heard a voice in my head and knew it was God. We never talked about God at my house, and I never went to church, but I knew it was God. And I knew that this place, with this beautiful light that was God, was my real home."[207]

Having studied the world's religious traditions and having friends who are members of diverse religious communities, I am convinced that no religious community should claim their spiritual experiences are the only truth. I hope their experiences are true for them, true in bringing into their lives the compassion and openness that truth requires. This is why I affirm, with all who defend the right to freedom of religion and belief, that authentic gifts of grace are open to all who feel called to respond.

I delight in Berry's insight that exploding supernova stars are "bestowers of grace." And I share his affirmation that, "This extravagant gift-giving is the spirituality of the universe. It is a form of cosmic love that enables the future to emerge."[208]

Finally, I endorse with process philosopher-theologian John Cobb, Jr. and physicist and out-of-body explorer Thomas Campbell, that while alive on earth we should focus our hearts and minds on helping to create and evolve an ecological civilization. Human greed and ignorance have caused the climate crisis that has led to numerous species extinctions and now threatens human survival. I explain and describe our crucial eco-choices in my university textbook, *Doing Environmental Ethics* (020) and also in other materials that are available on my website at *rtraer.com*.

May each of us respond creatively to the Light and Love calling us to sustain the biodiversity that has evolved on the earth.

---

207 Ibid, 80, 84,121.

208 Brian Swimme, *Cosmogenesis*, 295.

Index of Witnesses

Bibliography

Achterberg, Jeanne. *Imagery in Healing: Shamanism and Modern Medicine* (New Science Library, 1985).

Acosta-Urquidi, J. "Brainwaves and Heartwaves: Psychophysiological and Spiritual Dimensions of Energy Healing," *Journal of Alternative and Complementary Medicine* 10. No. 4 (2004):728.

Alcott, Louisa May. *Her Life, Letters, and Journals*, ed. Ednah Dow Littlehale Cheney (Little, Brown, and Company, 1919).

Alexander, Eben. "He said it: A neurosurgeon confronts the non-material nature of consciousness," *Uncommon Descent*, Dec. 2, 2011, https://uncommondescent.com/intelligent-design/he-said-it-a-neurosurgeon-confronts-the-non-material-nature-of-consciousness/.

Alexander, Eben. "My Experience in Coma," http://ebenalexander.com/about/my-experience-in-coma/. Accessed July 29, 2024.

Alexander, Eben. *Proof of Heaven: A Neurosurgeon's Journey into the Afterlife* (Simon & Schuster, 2012).

Amatuzio, Janis. *Beyond Knowing: Mysteries and Messages of Death and Life from a Forensic Pathologist* (New World Library, 2006).

Amatuzio, Janis. *Forever Ours: Real Stories of Immortality and Living from a Forensic Pathologist* (New World Library, 2004).

Anderson, Reggie. *Appointments with Heaven: The True Story of a Country Doctor's Healing Encounters with the Hereafter* (Tyndale House Publishers, 2013).

Baggott, Jim. *Farewell to Reality: How Modern Physics Has Betrayed the Search for Scientific Truth* (Pegasus Books, 2014).

Barušs, Imants and Julia Mossbridge. *Transcendent Mind: Rethinking the Science of Consciousness* (American Psychological Association, 2016).

Beauregard, Mario and Denyse O'Leary, *The Spiritual Brain: A Neuroscientist's Case for the Existence of the Soul*, (HarperOne, 2008).

Bellg, Laurin. *Near Death in the ICU: Stories from Patients Near Death and Why We Should Listen to Them* (Sloan Press, 2016), 1-12.

Blum, Deborah. *Ghost Hunters: William James and the Search for Scientific Proof of Life After Death* (Penguin, 2007).

Bohm, David. *Wholeness and the Implicate Order* (Routledge, 2002).

Campbell, Thomas. *My Big TOE [Theory of Everything]: A Trilogy Unifying Philosophy, Physics, and Metaphysics* (Lightning Strikes Books, 2003).

Chopra, Deepak. "Quantum Physics and Consciousness," in Karen Nesbitt Shanor, ed., *The Emerging Mind* (Renaissance Books, 1999).

Chopra, Deepak and Menas C. Kafatos. *You are the Universe: Discovering Your Cosmic Self and Why It Matters* (Harmony Books, 2017).

Chopra, Deepak. *Quantum Healing: Exploring the Frontiers of Mind/Body Healing* (Bantam, 2015).

Chopra, Deepak. *The Future of God: A Practical Approach to Spirituality for Our Times* (Harmony, 2014).

Chopra, Deepak and Sarah Platt-Finger. *Living in the Light* (Harmony/Rodale, Kindle Edition, 2023).

Cicoria, Tony. "The Electrifying Story of the Accidental Pianist & Composer," *Missouri Medicine*, 2014 Jul-Aug; 111(4): 308, https://www.ncbi.nlm.nih.gov/pmc/articles/PMC6179476/.

Dalai Lama, *The Universe in a Single Atom: The Convergence of Science and Spirituality* (Morgan Road Books, 2005).

Darling, David. *Soul Search: A Scientist Explores the Afterlife* (Villard Books, 1995).

Davies, Paul and John Gribbin. *The Matter Myth: Dramatic Discoveries that Challenge Our Understanding of Physical Reality* (Simon & Schuster, 1992).

Davies, Paul. *The Cosmic Blueprint: New Discoveries in Nature's Creative Ability to Order the Universe* (Templeton Press, 2004).

Davies, Paul. *The Goldilocks Enigma: Why is the Universe Just Right for Life?* (Mariner Books, 2008).

Deutsch, David. *The Beginning of Infinity: Explanations that Transform the World* (Penguin Books, 2012).

Dossey, Larry. *One Mind: How Our Individual Mind Is Part of a Greater consciousness and Why It Matters* (Hay House, 2013).

Doty, James R. *Into the Magic Shop: A Neurosurgeon's Quest to Discover the Mysteries of the Brain and the Secrets of the heart* (Avery, 2012), and https://ccare.stanford.edu/people/james-r-doty-md/.

Egnor, Michael. "Does Science Disprove Free Will? A Physicist Says No," *Mind Matters*, Nov 22, 2021, https://mindmatters.ai/2021/11/does-science-disprove-free-will-a-physicist-says-no/.

Fenwick, Peter and Elizabeth. *The Truth in the Light: An Investigation of Over 300 Near-Death Experiences* (Berkeley Books, 1997).

Fenwick, Peter, Hilary Lovelace, and Sue Brayne. "Comfort for the Dying: Five Year Retrospective and One Year Prospective Studies of End of Life Experiences," *Archives of Gerontology and Geriatrics* 51, no. 2 (September-October 2010): 4, https://a.edu/22946305/Comfort_for_the_dying_five_year_retrospective_and_one_year_prospective_studies_of_end_of_life_experiences.

Fenwick, Peter. *Shining Light on Transcendence: The Unconventional Journey of a Neuroscientist* (White Crow Books, Kindle Edition, 2019).

Galileo Commission Report, https://icrl.org/galileo-commission-report/.

Gefter, Amanda. "Near-Death Neurologist: Dreams on the Border of Life," *New Scientist*, Dec. 22, 2010; 2792:80-81.

Gibson, Leonard. "Amplified Subject," *Rethinking Consciousness: Extraordinary Consciousness: Extraordinary Challenges for Contemporary Science* (Process Century Press, 2020), https://processcenturypress.com/rethinking-consciousness-extraordinary-challenges-for-contemporary-science/.

Gingerich, Owen. *God's Universe* (Harvard University Press, 2016).

Greshko, Michael. "These Early Humans Lived 300,000 Years Ago—But Had Modern Faces," *National Geographic*, June 7, 2017, https://www.nationalgeographic.com/news/2017/06/morocco-early-human-fossils-anthropology-science/.

Greyson, Bruce. *After: A Doctor Explores What Near-Death Experiences Reveal about Life and Beyond* (St. Martin's Essentials, 2021).

Griffin, David Ray. *Reenchantment without Supernaturalism: A Process Philosophy of Religion* (Cornell University Press, 2001).

Grof, Stanislav. "The Revision and Re-Enchantment of Psychology: The Legacy of Half a Century of Consciousness Research," https://galileocomission.org/revision-and-re-enchantment-of-psychology-legacy-of-half-a-century-of-consciousness-research-grof-2012/.

Grosso, Michael. *The Final Choice: Playing the Survival Game* (Stillpoint Publishing, 1985).

Hamilton, Allan J. *The Scalpel and the Soul: Encounters with Surgery, the Supernatural, and the Healing Power of Hope* (Penguin, 2009).

Hawkes, Joyce Whiteley. *Cell-Level Healing The Bridge from Soul to Cell (Atria Paperback, 2006.*

Hawkes, Joyce Whiteley. "Cell-Level Healing: Where Science and Spirit Meet," https://celllevelhealing.com/.

Hoffman, David D. *The Case Against Reality: Why Evolution Hid the Truth from Our Eyes* (W. W. Norton & Company. Kindle Edition, 2019).

"Intuition Quotes," *Today in Science History*, https://todayinsci.com/Quotations Categories/I_Cat/Intuition-Quotations.htm. Accessed March 23, 2021.

"Investigation of George Ritchie's NDE OBE," updated February 18, 2010, https://www.selfconsciousmind.com/ritchie/.

Jackson, Laura Lynne. *The Light Between Us: Stories from Heaven* (Spiegal & Grau, 2015).

Johnston Catherine and Rebecca Nappi, "EndNotes: A Nurse's Tale: The Spirit Leaves the Body," *Spokesman-Review*, July 12, 2012, https://www.spokesman.com/blogs/endnotes/2012/jul/12/nurses-tale-spirit-leaves-body.

Jung, Carl Gustav. *Memories, Dreams, Reflections* (Vintage Books, 1989).

Kaku, Michio. *The Future of the Mind: The Scientific Quest to Understand, Enhance, and Empower the Mind (Anchor, 2014).*

Kauffman, Stuart A. Reinventing the Sacred: *A New View of Science, Reason, and Religion* (Basic Books, 2010).

Kelly, Edward and Emily Kelly. *Irreducible Mind: Toward a Psychology for the 21st Century* (Rowman & Littlefield, 2009).

Kerr, Christopher and Carine Mardorossian. *Death is But a Dream: Finding Hope and Meaning at Life's End*, (Penguin Publishing, 2020).

Kircher, Pamela M. *Love Is the Link: A Hospice Doctor Shares Her Experience of Near-Death and Dying* (Awakenings Press, 2013).

Lanza, Robert and Bob Berman. *Beyond Biocentrism: Rethinking Time Space, Consciousness, and the Illusion of Death* (BenBella Books, 2016).

Lewin, R. "Is Your Brain Really Necessary?" *Science* 210 (1980): 1232-34.

Libet, Benjamin. *Mind Time: The Temporal Factor in Consciousness* (Harvard University Press, 2004).

Long, Jeffrey and Paul Perry. *God and the Afterlife: The Groundbreaking New Evidence for God and Near-Death Experience* (HarperOne, 2016).

Long, Jeffrey Long and Paul Perry. *Evidence of the Afterlife: The Science of Near-Death Experiences* (HarperOne, 2010).

Louie, A. H. "Robert Rosen's Anticipatory Systems," January 2010, https://www.researchgate.net/publication/228091658_Robert_Rosen's_anticipatory_systems.

Manifesto for a Post-Materialist Science, https://opensciences.org/about/manifesto-for-a-post-materialist-science?

Martial, Charlotte, Héléna Cassol, and Vanessa Charland-Verville, et al., "Neurochemical Models of Near-Death Experiences: A Large-Scale Study Based on the Semantic Similarity of Written Reports," *Consciousness and Cognition* 69 (2019), 52-69.

Mayer, Elizabeth Lloyd. *Extraordinary Knowing: Science, Skepticism, and the Inexplicable Powers of the Human Mind* (Bantam Books, 2007).

Mayer, Elizabeth Lloyd. https://www.penguinrandomhouse.com/books/109557/extraordinary-knowing-by-elizabeth-lloyd-mayer-phd/. Accessed July 27, 2024.

Miller, Kenneth R. *Finding Darwin's God: A Scientist's Search for Common Ground Between God and Evolution (Harper Perennial, 2007).*

Monroe Institute, https://www.monroeinstitute.org/.

Moody, Raymond A. and Paul Perry. *Glimpses of Eternity: An Investigation into Shared Death* (Rider, 2010).

Moody, Raymond A. and Paul Perry. *Paranormal: My Life in Pursuit of the Afterlife* (HarperOne, 2012).

Moody, Raymond A. and Paul Perry, *Proof of Life After Life: 7 Reasons to Believe There Is an Afterlife* (Atria books/Beyond Words, 2023).

Moody, Raymond A. and Paul Perry. *Reunions: Visionary Encounters with Departed Loved Ones* (Villard Books, 1993).

Morse, Melvin and Paul Perry. *Parting Visions: Uses and Meanings of Pre-Death, Psychic, and Spiritual Experiences* (Villard Books 1994).

Nagel, Thomas. *Mind and Cosmos: Why the Materialist Neo-Darwinian Conception of Nature is Almost Certainly False* (Oxford University Press, 2012).

Noë, Alva. *Out of Our Heads: Why You Are Not Your Brain and Other Lessons from the Biology of Consciousness* (Hill and Wang, 2009).

Olsen, Jeff and Jeff O'Driscoll. "Their Shared Near-Death Experience Formed an Unbreakable Bond," *Guideposts*, https://guideposts.org/amgels-and-miracles/life-after-death/their-shared-near-death-experience-formed-an-unbreakable-bond; and an interview with Paul Perry in 1999.

Ossowiecki, Stefan. https://allaboutheaven.org/sources/ossowiecki-stefan/190.

Parti, Raj and Paul Perry. *Dying to Wake Up: A Doctor's Voyage into the Afterlife and the Wisdom He brought Back* (Simon & Schuster, 2017).

Penfield, Wilder. *The Mystery of the Mind: A Critical Study of Consciousness and the Human Brain* (Princeton University Press, 1975).

Planck, Max. https://bigthink.com/words-of-wisdom/max-planck-i-regard-consciousness-as-fundamental. Accessed August 15, 2024.

Rockwell, Teed W. *Neither Brain Nor Ghost: A Nondualist Alternative to the Mind-Brain Identity Theory* (Bradford Book, 2007).

Russell, Peter. "Ripples of Knowing," https://www.peterrussell.com/SP/conscrising.php. Accessed August 23, 2024.

Rynes, Nancy. https://www.nancyrynes.com/my-story. Accessed March 10, 2021.

Rynes, Nancy. https://www.nderf.org/Experiences/1nancy_r_ndes.html. Accessed August 2,2024.

Sacks, Oliver. "A Bolt from the Blue," *The New Yorker*, July 16, 2007, https://www.newyorker.com/magazine/2007/07/23/a-bolt-from-the-blue.

Schlitz, Marilyn. *Death Makes Life Possible: Revolutionary Insights on Living, Dying, and the Continuation of Consciousness* (Sounds True, 2015).

Schwartz, Stephan A. *The Secret Vaults of Time: Psychic Archaeology and the Quest for Man's Beginnings* (Open Road Distribution, 2017).

Sheldrake, Rupert. *The Rebirth of Nature: The Greening of Science and God* (Park Street Press, 1991, 1994).

Siegel, Bernie S. and Cynthia J. Hurn. *The Art of Healing: Uncovering Your Inner Wisdom and Potential for Self-Healing* (New World Library, 2013).

Simpson, Mona. "A Sister's Eulogy for Steve Jobs," *The New York Times*, Oct. 30, 2011, https://www.nytimes.com/2011/10/30/opinion/mona-simpsons-eulogy-for-steve-jobs.html.

Sosteric, Mike. "Mysticism, Consciousness, Death," *Journal of Consciousness Exploration & Research*, Dec. 2016, vol. 7, issue 11, 1099-1118.

Sosteric, Mike. "Three Interesting Things Einstein Said About God and Religion," *The Lightning Strike*, Sep. 12, 2019, https://medium.com/human-spirituality/three-interesting-things-einstein-said-about-god-and-religion-11798a4e23d7.

Sosteric, Mike. *Rocket Scientists' Guide to Authentic Spirituality* (Lightning Path Press, 2010).

Swimme, Brian Thomas. *Cosmogenesis* (Catapult, Kindle Edition, 2022).

Swimme, Brian Thomas and Mary Evelyn Tucker. *Journey of the Universe* (Yale University Press, 2011).

Targ, Rusell. *Limitless Mind: A Guide to Remote Viewing and Transformation of Consciousness* (New World Library, 2010).

Thompson, Evan. *Mind in Life: Biology, Phenomenology, and the Sciences of Mind* (Belknap Press: An Imprint of Harvard University Press, 2010).

Tompkins, Ptolemy. *The Modern Book of the Dead* (Atria Books, 2012).

Traer, Robert. Widening Our Compassion, *https://rtraer.com.*

Umoh, Ruth. "Steve Jobs and Albert Einstein both attributed their extraordinary success to this personality trait," CNBC: *MakeIt*, Jan.29, 2017, https://www.cnbc.com/2017/06/29/steve-jobs-and-albert-einstein-both-attributed-their-extraordinary-success-to-this-personality-trait.html.

van Lommel, Pim. *Consciousness Beyond Life: The Science of the Near-Death Experience* (HarperOne, 2010).

van Lommel, Pim. https://pimvanlommel.nl/en/pim-van-lommel/biography/. Accessed July 29, 2024.

van Lommel, Pim. *Journal of Consciousness Studies*, 20, Ni. 1-2, 2013, 39.

van Lommel, Pim. "Near-Death Experiences: The Experience of the Self as Real and Not as an Illusion," *Annals N.Y. Academy of Sciences*, 2011, ISSN 0077-8923.

Vlastos, Gregory. *Studies in Greek Philosophy*, vol. 2 (Princeton University Press, 1995).

Walker, Evan Harris. *The Physics of Consciousness: The Quantum Mind and the Meaning of Life* (Perseus Books, 2000).

Whitehead, Alfred North. *Process and Reality* (Free Press, 2010).

Wilson, E. O. *Consilience: The Unity of Knowledge* (Vintage Books, 1999).

Yates, Jenny, ed. *Jung on Death and Immortality* (Princeton University Press, 1999).